C000149779

WHERE THE WORLD MEETS TO PRAY

Sarah Wilke
Publisher

INTERDENOMINATIONAL
INTERNATIONAL
INTERRACIAL

77 EDITIONS
35 LANGUAGES

The Upper Room
May–August 2014
Edited by Susan Hibbins

The Upper Room © BRF 2014
The Bible Reading Fellowship
15 The Chambers, Vineyard, Abingdon OX14 3FE
Tel: 01865 319700; Fax: 01865 319701
Email: enquiries@brf.org.uk
Website: www.brf.org.uk
BRF is a Registered Charity

ISBN 978 0 85746 039 4

Acknowledgments
The New Revised Standard Version of the Bible, Anglicised edition, copyright © 1989, 1995 by the Division of Christian Education of the National Council of the Churches of Christ in the USA. Used by permission. All rights reserved.

The Holy Bible, New International Version (Anglicised edition), copyright © 1979, 1984, 2011 by Biblica (formerly International Bible Society). Used by permission of Hodder & Stoughton Publishers, an Hachette UK company. All rights reserved. 'NIV' is a registered trademark of Biblica (formerly International Bible Society). UK trademark number 1448790.

Extracts from the Authorised Version of the Bible (The King James Bible), the rights in which are vested in the Crown, are reproduced by permission of the Crown's Patentee, Cambridge University Press.

Extracts from CEB copyright © 2011 by Common English Bible.

Printed by Gutenberg Press, Tarxien, Malta.

The Upper Room: how to use this book

The Upper Room is ideal in helping us spend a quiet time with God each day. Each daily entry is based on a passage of scripture, and is followed by a meditation and prayer. Each person who contributes a meditation to the magazine seeks to relate their experience of God in a way that will help those who use The Upper Room every day.

Here are some guidelines to help you make best use of The Upper Room:

1. Read the passage of Scripture. It is a good idea to read it more than once, in order to have a fuller understanding of what it is about and what you can learn from it.
2. Read the meditation. How does it relate to your own experience? Can you identify with what the writer has outlined from their own experience or understanding?
3. Pray the written prayer. Think about how you can use it to relate to people you know, or situations that need your prayers today.
4. Think about the contributor who has written the meditation. Some Upper Room users include this person in their prayers for the day.
5. Meditate on the 'Thought for the Day', the 'Link2Life' and the 'Prayer Focus', perhaps using them again as the focus for prayer or direction for action.

Why is it important to have a daily quiet time? Many people will agree that it is the best way of keeping in touch every day with the God who sustains us, and who sends us out to do his will and show his love to the people we encounter each day. Meeting with God in this way reassures us of his presence with us, helps us to discern his will for us and makes us part of his worldwide family of Christian people through our prayers.

I hope that you will be encouraged as you use the magazine regularly as part of your daily devotions, and that God will richly bless you as you read his word and seek to learn more about him.

Susan Hibbins
UK Editor

Below is a list of entries in this copy of *The Upper Room* relating to situations or emotions with which we may need help:

Anger: May 19

Addiction: Aug 23

Anxiety: May 25; Jun 27

Assurance: May 10, 26; Jun 29; Jul 10, 15; Aug 12, 28

Bible reading: May 7, 28; Jun 3, 12; Jul 11, 16; Aug 5, 6

Change: May 1; Jun 11, 21

Christian community: May 3, 19, 26; Jun 1, 25; Jul 1, 6, 18; Aug 13

Compassion: May 27, 29; Jul 4

Creation/nature's beauty: May 1, 5, 9; Jun 27; Jul 14; Aug 18, 19

Death/grief: Jun 21; Jul 5

Discouragement: Jul 17

Doubt: Jul 15; Aug 8

Encouragement: May 3, 22; Jun 1, 25; Jul 28; Aug 13

Family: May 12; Jun 14, 15; Aug 4, 20

Fear: May 21; Jun 9, 17; Jul 9, 29

Financial concerns: May 25; Jun 4; Aug 14, 17

Forgiveness: May 12, 24; Jun 29; Jul 5, 18, 22; Aug 30

Friendship: Jun 4, 25; Jul 18, 25; Aug 27

Generosity/giving: May 17, 22; Jun 7, 28; Jul 4; Aug 14

God's goodness/love: May 20; Jun 12, 14, 29; Jul 27, 30; Aug 4, 28

God's presence: May 4, 23; Jun 6, 17, 27; Jul 3, 7, 11; Aug 3, 31

God's provision: May 5; Jul 8, 19, 26, 28

Gratitude: May 1, 15, 31; Jun 28; Aug 7, 15, 26

Growth: May 14, 27; Jul 20, 31

Guidance: Jun 3, 30; Jul 30; Aug 5, 7, 9

Healing/illness: May 4, 29; Jun 12, 26; Jul 23; Aug 11, 26, 31

Hope: Jul 28; Aug 31

Job issues: Jul 12; Aug 12

Judging: Jul 2; Aug 21

Living our faith: May 27; Jun 1, 3, 4; Jul 2, 3, 16; Aug 6

Loneliness: May 11; Jul 26; Aug 16

Loss: May 17

Mental illness: May 8; Jun 2, 18, 26; Jul 10; Aug 20, 23

Mission/outreach: May 30; Jun 2, 7, 13; Jul 4, 29; Aug 10

New beginnings: Jun 11; Jul 20, 27; Aug 18, 20

Parenting: May 2, 11, 14; Jun 15

Patience: Jun 18

Peace/unrest: May 19

Prayer: May 2, 31; Jun 2, 13, 16; Jul 1, 25; Aug 8, 27

Renewal: Jun 24; Jul 13, 24; Aug 24

Repentance: Jun 24, 29; Aug 1, 30

Salvation: May 12, 30; Jun 8, 22; Jul 22; Aug 17

Security: May 11; Jun 17; Aug 2

Serving: May 3, 18, 20, 29; Jun 10, 11, 20, 22

Speaking about faith: May 8, 28; Jun 4

Social issues: Jun 10, 16

Spiritual gifts: May 3, 6, 15; Jun 20, 28; Aug 10

Spiritual practices: May 5, 28; Jun 9, 19, 30; Jul 8, 31; Aug 1, 29

Stewardship: Aug 14

Strength: May 16; Jun 21; Jul 21

Stress: Aug 4, 19

Tolerance: Jun 19

Tragedy: May 10, 26

Trust: May 2, 25; Jun 7; Jul 12, 21; Aug 3, 9

'Do not be frightened, and do not be dismayed, for the Lord your God is with you wherever you go' (Joshua 1:9).

I noticed this fellow traveller almost immediately after we stepped off the plane from New York. Her face was as worried as it was weary. 'Where are the bags?' she asked me in halting English. I pointed her toward a baggage-claim sign, but I quickly saw this wasn't enough. 'Come on,' I said. 'We'll go together.'

I was on familiar turf—Nashville, my home airport—but all of my international travel for *The Upper Room* has taught me well how it feels to be a stranger in a strange land. As we walked, I learned the woman had been travelling for 24 hours from Russia. In the United States for the first time, she was here to visit a daughter she hadn't seen in ten years. I also learned of another anxiety: she wasn't sure her daughter knew where to find her at the airport.

While we awaited the luggage, I helped the woman to telephone her daughter, who was on her way, and I arranged a meeting place. But still, the woman's uneasiness persisted. 'Don't worry,' I said. 'I will stay with you until your daughter comes.' She looked puzzled, and I repeated the words. Once she comprehended, she finally relaxed.

The hug this stranger gave me as she got in her daughter's car told me how much my presence had meant to her. What I offered was small—just a few brief minutes of my time—but what God offers us is every moment of every day. Wherever we go, we are assured that the steadfast presence of his love will see us through every fear of the unknown.

Sarah Wilke
Publisher

The Upper Room has been published in the United Kingdom for 60 years. Since 2009 the magazine has been in partnership with The Bible Reading Fellowship (BRF), an organisation that produces spiritual formation resources. Despite the decline of Christian retailers in the UK, *The Upper Room* continues to grow in its readership of about 8,000.

Over the years, the United Kingdom edition of *The Upper Room* has been diligent in recruiting and cultivating writers for the magazine. In July 2012, the UK edition editor, Susan Hibbins, led the first Writers' Day sponsored by BRF in England. During the event, participants explored devotional writing and learned more about *The Upper Room*'s publishing processes. Susan has seen the difference this magazine can make in people's lives. Through events like Writers' Day, she hopes people will learn to 'write in such a way that the power of scripture will extend beyond their writing and reach many people'.

In March 2013, leaders from BRF visited the Upper Room offices in Nashville, Tennessee, to help them understand and appreciate even more the ministry of The Upper Room. Hearing people talk about their work and the prayer that goes into the preparation of each issue of the magazine enabled participants to capture the vision for this important work.

We invite you to pray with us for the readers of *The Upper Room* in the United Kingdom and around the world that those who read this magazine will grow in faith and Christian discipleship.

To learn more about the UK-English edition, go to international.upperroom.org/europe/theunitedkingdom-englishedition

The Editor writes...

'Praise the Lord.'

This is the first verse of Psalm 111, an acrostic poem in which each line begins with successive letters of the Hebrew alphabet. It formed part of my devotional reading last year. As it is a psalm of praise that details some of the many blessings God has bestowed, the writer of the commentary I was using suggested that we could use the example of the psalm to compile our own 'alphabet of praise'.

Where would you start? There are so many things to praise God for, and to list them alphabetically concentrates the mind, instead of praising him for all his blessings in a blanket way. My list would include people I love who have enriched my understanding and helped me in hard times; places I have visited, the pastimes I enjoy; the wonders and beauties I see all around me and the senses he has given me to enjoy them; good health; family... as you can see, the list goes on and on.

As part of our daily prayer life, praise helps us to focus on everything that is good, rather than the opposite. We are fed a daily diet of bad news, and the troubles of the world—its wars, famines, unrest and injustices—can permeate our consciousness until we feel overwhelmed. While it is important to do as much as we can in all of this, it also helps if we remember to praise God for the good things: for all those who seek to do good in bad situations; for those, largely unsung, who give time and effort in local situations to help other people; for those who take God's love to the lonely and ill.

On a personal level, too, it helps, if we're feeling depressed by the way life is going, to try to praise God for all he has done for us. Remembering all our blessings in the past reassures for the present and gives us hope for the future.

Praise the Lord!

Susan Hibbins
Editor of the UK edition

Change

Read Psalm 98:1–6

Shout for joy to the Lord.
Psalm 98:4 (NIV)

Early in May I was talking with a neighbour who was disappointed that the leaves of his maple tree hadn't yet changed colour. Within a few days of our conversation we experienced three successive frosts, our first for the year. Suddenly, my neighbour's tree, along with thousands of others in the area, changed dramatically. They took on the oranges, reds and deep gold colours that had been missing throughout our mild autumn. Driving around our streets became such a delight as the trees suddenly blazed with colour and seemed to shimmer as gentle breezes stirred within the leaves.

Normally I dislike the start of the frosty winter season, but this year it brought such a complete change in the foliage that I was able to rejoice in the amazing beauty of God's creation.

So often I'm ready to see the downside of changes occurring around me but fail to remember to thank God as I also begin to see the benefits of the changes. This autumn I felt nurtured, as God gently showed me how all of creation works together to create beauty and wonder. It deepened my trust in him and helped me to learn to look for reasons to rejoice in everything I experience.

Prayer: *Wonderful, creative God, thank you for all the blessings you shower upon us. Help us to rejoice with you in the beauty and the good in all you give us. Amen*

Thought for the day: Today I will rejoice in the beauty of creation.

Meg Mangan (New South Wales, Australia)

PRAYER FOCUS: TO LOOK FOR THE BEAUTY AROUND US

Faith of a Child

Read Mark 10:13–16
Whoever does not receive the kingdom of God as a little child will never enter it.
Mark 10:15 (NRSV)

When my daughter was four she came to me with a broken toy and asked me to mend it. Often when she would 'break' her toys I would be able to snap or glue a piece back on. However, this time she had snapped a piece in half. 'I'm sorry, sweetheart, I can't mend this,' I told her. She responded, 'Mummy, let's pray to Jesus to mend it.' How do you explain that the toy will still be broken to a child who believes that Jesus can do anything? Yet, when I told her that we could pray but that Jesus probably was not going to mend her toy, she simply responded, 'Let's pray anyway.'

At that moment I understood why Jesus told his disciples that to enter the kingdom of heaven you must become like a little child (Mark 10:15; Matthew 18:3). At the age of four, my daughter understood that God loves us and wants us to pray even if we do not think we are going to get the answer we want.

I often think I need to handle my problems on my own, that they are too small for God. However, my daughter reminded me that nothing is too small for him. He wants us to lay all our burdens down and trust in his love for us.

Prayer: *Dear loving God, help us remember that nothing is too small to bring to you in prayer. Help us bring all of our burdens to you with the faith of a child. Amen*

Thought for the day: Today I will pray with the faith of a child.

Debbie Herrington (Michigan, US)

Unsung Heroes

Read John 1:35–42

One of the two who heard John speak and followed him was Andrew, Simon Peter's brother.

John 1:40 (NRSV)

I recently read a book that outlined the lives of Jesus' twelve disciples. I was especially interested to learn about Andrew. As today's scripture points out, he introduced his brother Peter to Christ, and Peter turned out to be the leader of the disciples. But all of that happened because of what Andrew did. To me, Andrew was an unsung hero among the disciples.

The Bible certainly has its 'star players', the ones we hear about often in the Old and New Testament. But our heritage of faith also includes the less well-known players, like Andrew, who play an important role without receiving as much attention.

Our role in serving God may receive lots of attention, and there's nothing wrong with that. But when it comes to serving the Lord, all roles are important—even those that seem to be minor. The apostle Paul summed it up well in his letter to the Colossians: 'Whatever you do, work at it with all your heart… It is the Lord Christ you are serving' (3:23, 24, NIV). That's a great reminder for us all.

Prayer: *Dear God, thank you for those who do your work without expecting recognition from others. Help us to remember that the work we do is your work. Amen*

Thought for the day: God calls us to serve even when we don't receive recognition.

John D. Bown (Minnesota, US)

Be Still

Read Psalm 46:1–11
Whoever dwells in the shelter of the Most High will rest in the shadow of the Almighty.
Psalm 91:1 (NIV)

Working in a small cottage hospital I see and hear many things. Most of those who come in for care are elderly. Some of our patients are with us because of a fall. Some come to us for help with chronic diseases such as Parkinson's. During visiting hours one afternoon I observed a patient's daughter sitting with her mother face-to-face next to her bed. No word was spoken throughout their time together, yet it did not seem at all awkward. I assumed that they had shared so much of each other's lives over so many years that they could sit there in silence, comfortably safe and content in each other's company.

This scene made me think of how I fill my life and prayers with unnecessary words and often miss the opportunity simply to be in God's presence. As I watched that mother and daughter sit together, Psalm 46:10 spoke to me clearly: 'Be still, and know that I am God; I will be exalted among the nations, I will be exalted in the earth' (NIV).

Prayer: *We praise you, dear Lord, for your constant presence. Help us to quiet our lives and understand the awesome beauty of spending time in your presence. Amen*

Thought for the day: We are invited to be still in God's presence.

Gina Matthews (Hampshire, England)

Gardening with God

Read John 15:1–8
Grow in the grace and knowledge of our Lord and Saviour Jesus Christ.
To him be glory both now and forever!
2 Peter 3:18 (NIV)

A new gardener, I admired my lush tomato plants. Their green foliage and bright yellow blossoms promised delicious tomatoes. One evening, a local vegetable grower stopped and looked at my garden. 'These are suckers,' he said, pointing to stray stems on my tomatoes. 'Cut them off. They're a haven for diseases and pests, and they take energy away from producing tomatoes.' I got out my clippers and pruned. Then I groaned in disgust as my efforts revealed caterpillars! They had been hiding in the dense leaves, munching away and destroying my plants.

Jesus warned his disciples about the need for pruning to help a plant bear more fruit: 'I am the true vine, and my Father is the gardener. He cuts off every branch in me that bears no fruit, while every branch that does bear fruit he prunes so that it will be even more fruitful' (John 15:1–2, NIV).

The Master Gardener wants me to prune what is unproductive in my life so I can pour my energy into bearing fruit. If I trim away bad habits and cut out activities that diminish my service, I can reduce opportunities for sin to creep into my life unnoticed. That way I can be a fruitful servant in God's kingdom.

Prayer: *Dear Lord, thank you for planting your word in our hearts. Help us to grow in Christ and to bear fruit in your kingdom. Amen*

Thought for the day: I want to stay connected to Christ so I can bloom and grow.

Keri Lewis (Mississippi, US)

In Times of Trouble

Read Psalm 46

God is our refuge and strength, a very present help in trouble.
Psalm 46:1 (NRSV)

On a cold winter's evening my son left me to babysit his two young children while he went to collect his wife from work. The children were in bed, but called out to me to say that they were afraid; the wind outside was howling and rattling the window-frames. I went into their room and settled them back to bed, and then I sat with them for a while until they went to sleep.

This made me remember that it is the same with God; we call on him when there are storms in our lives and we too are afraid. Our loving God will be there to share our problems with us.

I didn't take away the noise of the wind for my grandchildren but they trusted in my presence and were comforted by it. Likewise God may not take away the problems we have to face, but if we ask him he will be at our side to ride out our storms with us.

Prayer: *Dear God, thank you for caring for us, and thank you too for sending us help in times of trouble. Amen*

Thought for the day: Could we be the help that God is sending to our neighbour?

Edith McLaughlin (Lanarkshire, Scotland)

Praying Like Paul and Harold

Read Colossians 1:9–14
Devote yourselves to prayer, being watchful and thankful.
Colossians 4:2 (NIV)

Harold was a member of our small group who loved God and was passionate about serving. He was an older man with godly wisdom and was much respected and appreciated by our group.

When we prayed together and for each other I noticed a difference between Harold's prayers and my own. My prayers often sounded like a shopping list of requests. Harold's prayers were more like the prayers of Paul and others who are found in the Bible. Paul and Harold prayed for spiritual blessings for others. They prayed for things that really got to the core of people's needs, so that those prayed for would grow and develop characters that would be more Christ-like.

I now use the Bible more when I pray for others and myself. The prayers in scripture are very beautiful and encouraging, like the one in the first chapter of Colossians. My prayer life has been deepened as I have used the Bible to shape my prayers. I often find that God directs me to the right verse to pray to meet a specific need.

I will be forever grateful to Harold for teaching me this powerful way to add strength and purpose to my prayers.

Prayer: *Thank you, dear Father, for the power of your word. Continue to show us how to use it as we pray. Amen*

Thought for the day: God's word gives guidance and purpose as we pray.

Ann Stewart (South Australia, Australia)

God's Faithfulness to Us

Read 2 Timothy 2:8–13

If we are faithless, [Christ] remains faithful—for he cannot deny himself.
2 Timothy 2:13 (NRSV)

Looking at Sarah, I could hardly believe this was the same woman I had known earlier. Now she was in a psychiatric ward at the hospital suffering with deep depression. Her eyes were heavy and red. This woman who had always been deeply faithful was telling me in a low and tearful voice, 'I don't think God cares about me anymore. I'm not sure I even believe anymore.'

Had this been a week earlier, I would have struggled to find words that would give her assurance that God did indeed care about her, that she should continue to trust God with her life. I would have tried to find any words that would lighten some of the pain she was experiencing. But it happened that just days before, I came across 2 Timothy 2:13 in my devotional reading. At the time, the words were a virtuous thought, but they didn't really speak to me—until I visited Sarah and the words came alive. The verse spoke directly to Sarah's condition: 'If we are faithless, Christ remains faithful—for he cannot deny himself.'

As I left Sarah with those words, I saw a ray of hope on her face. I praised the Holy Spirit for leading me to the right place with the right message of God's love and faithfulness to us all.

Prayer: *Thank you, dear Lord, for your faithfulness to us. We are sometimes too weak to come to you with our concerns. But you know what they are and you care for us. Amen*

Thought for the day: Even when we doubt, Christ remains faithful.

Betty Rosian (Pennsylvania, US)

Miraculous Bodies

Read Ephesians 4:11–16

From [Christ], the whole body, joined and knitted together by every ligament with which it is equipped… promotes the body's growth in building itself up in love.
Ephesians 4:15–16 (NRSV)

I was coming to the end of an incredibly stressful term at college when one day I awoke face-down on the floor of my college hallway. Luckily for me, as I would find out, what had happened was a relatively common form of fainting brought about by fatigue and dehydration. A very simple thing—the misfiring of one nerve—led to my passing out. It was a reminder of how incredibly complicated and miraculous our bodies are. Each is unique. Each has different challenges, struggles and pains; but each body also has special beauty. The more that modern science tells us about how our bodies function, the more miraculous they seem.

In a similar way the body of Christ is a miracle. Despite our many differences, we somehow work together to do the work of Christ in the world. In today's reading, Paul describes the body of Christ in vivid detail, knit together by ligaments of love. Our striving together is a miracle of love. In spite of our human frailties, God is not distant from us but works alongside and through us to do truly amazing things.

Prayer: *Dear God, thank you for the gift of our bodies. Please empower us to use them to further the message of Jesus. Amen*

Thought for the day: The body God gave me is a good and beautiful thing.

David Hosey (Washington DC, US)

Such Great Love

Read Lamentations 3:22–26

The steadfast love of the Lord never ceases, his mercies never come to an end.

Lamentations 3:22 (NRSV)

The morning my husband left me, I felt hurt and helpless. He had been depressed for several days, and I had been praying for him for months. I loved him; but I knew it was time to let him go and to entrust him to God.

I felt a profound sense of loneliness, to the point of feeling diminished. I prayed, and I know our lives will work out in time. I believe in God's promises and love, but that afternoon I felt a deep sadness.

Then I felt God assuring me: 'You are truly loved. I am here. This crisis will pass.'

Jesus Christ is always present in the most difficult crises and in circumstances of grave pain and anguish. I belong to Christ even as I experience this heartbreaking situation. I will continue to believe in him, and I rejoice that I am a beloved child of God.

Prayer: *Dear God of love and mercy, help us to turn our troubles and grief over to you and to give you the glory, as we pray, 'Our Father which art in heaven, Hallowed be thy name. Thy kingdom come. Thy will be done, as in heaven, so in earth. Give us day by day our daily bread. And forgive us our sins; for we also forgive every one that is indebted to us. And lead us not into temptation; but deliver us from evil.'* In the name of your Son, we pray. Amen*

Thought for the day: God's love will never let us go.

Mercedes Zaragoza (Mexico)

PRAYER FOCUS: HUSBANDS AND WIVES WHO SEPARATE   17

* Luke 11:2–4 (KJV)

The Mother Heart of God

Read Psalm 131:1–3

As a mother comforts her child, so will I comfort you.
Isaiah 66:13 (NIV)

'Mummy!' My daughter's middle-of-the-night whimper drags me from my cocoon of sleep. She is up yet again with a flu bug that won't leave her alone, even at two in the morning. Her cries awaken compassion in my sleepy heart, and I use my gentlest touch and my softest voice to make her comfortable again. I pull her blanket up, smoothing her hair with my hand. 'Go to sleep now,' I soothe. 'Everything's all right.' She sighs contentedly and closes her eyes.

Back in my own bed, I remember a phrase: the mother heart of God. I have heard the phrase before, but tonight I understand it in a new way. It means I am not alone. I feel alone sometimes. When I am the one with the flu or when I wake up in the dark after a bad dream, I long for my mother's presence and help. I still need her, even though I am 35 and years gone from her house. I think I will always need her special love and protection. It comforts me to think that, although my earthly mother is not at my bedside tonight, God, with the heart of a mother, listens for my cry. God whispers, 'Go back to sleep now. Everything's all right. I'm here.'

Prayer: *Help us to depend on you, dear God, as a child depends on his or her mother. Amen*

Thought for the day: God tends to us as a mother tends to her child.

Sara Matson (Minnesota, US)

The Gift

Read Ephesians 2:1–10

It is by grace you have been saved, through faith—and this not from yourselves, it is the gift of God.

Ephesians 2:8 (NIV)

After a childhood bout of rheumatic fever, my mother did not expect to survive into her teens, much less marry and have children. But she lived well into her sixties and welcomed 21 grandchildren into the family. As the youngest of six children, I watched my mother make tiny baby clothes each time one of her daughters or daughters-in-law announced an impending birth.

Six years after my mother's death, my oldest sister visited. She gave us a present to celebrate the long-awaited news of our impending parenthood. Smiling, she said the gift was from my mother. Startled, we opened the gift from someone who no longer lived on earth, but who loved us and our unborn daughter. Mum had lovingly fashioned new baby clothes and left them with my sister to give to us at the right time.

Mum's gift reminded me that Jesus offers each of us the gift of forgiveness and eternal life—even many centuries after his death. No gift can be redeemed until it is accepted. Let our acts of giving, whether of time or talent, be a strong reminder of the gift given to us by someone who died many years ago.

Prayer: *Dear Lord, thank you for giving us so much when we have done nothing to deserve it. Amen*

Thought for the day: No gift compares to the gift of salvation.

Jerry Maurer (California, US)

PRAYER FOCUS: THOSE AWAITING THE BIRTH OF A CHILD

Going for the Goal

Read Hebrews 12:1–3

'Forgetting what is behind and straining toward what is ahead, I press on toward the goal.'
Philippians 3:13–14 (NIV)

Every summer, cyclists from Britain and abroad arrive to take part in a 70-mile rally along the country roads in the area where I live, which starts and ends outside our church. This year, on my way to morning worship, I mingled with the people who had gathered. What excitement! Adults and children shouted, waved and jumped whenever weary competitors crossed the finishing line. A piper in full Highland dress welcomed them. The cyclists were relieved and delighted as they completed the long, hard route.

Later, I reflected on that scene and recognised how clearly it illustrated Hebrews 12:1–3. The cyclists travelled light. Nothing slowed them down; even their clothes were body-tight. As they set off, they had a single aim: to complete the course, whatever challenges it presented.

We may not be cyclists or runners, but all who belong to Jesus are in a race together. Let us encourage one another not to get sidetracked or to give up. Instead, let us fix our eyes on Jesus, who knows from experience each challenge we face. He guides us to the finishing line, where a 'great cloud of witnesses' (Hebrews 12:1) waits to cheer us home!

Prayer: *Dear Lord Jesus, help us to fix our eyes on you and encourage one another to finish the race. Amen*

Thought for the day: As Christians, we are all in this race together.

Elaine M. Brown (Perthshire, Scotland)

Blessed by Autism

Read 2 Corinthians 1:3–7

Blessed be the God... of all consolation, who consoles us in all our affliction.
2 Corinthians 1:3–4 (NRSV)

Our son was diagnosed with autism when he was two years old. My wife noticed subtle changes in his behaviour; within months, his language and social interactions became severely diminished. The outgoing boy we knew and loved was gone, fixed in his own world. Nothing could have prepared us for what we were facing. We turned to God, praying for our son's recovery. Knowing that a complete recovery would be uncommon, we also prayed for our understanding and acceptance.

We found a private school that serves children with autism. After six months, our son has changed significantly. We have been able to rally around our son as he continues to progress a little each day, one step at a time. By concentrating on intervention and progress, we have developed a healthy perspective toward his condition. We are involved in a healing process, emotionally for our family and developmentally for our child. Now even the smallest improvement feels like the biggest blessing. I firmly believe that through this sudden adversity, we've been brought closer to God and to one another.

Prayer: *O Lord, may we be strengthened by adversities and feel your loving presence with us always. Amen*

Thought for the day: Small improvements can be big blessings.

Anthony Castellitto (New Jersey, US)

Paying Attention

Read Colossians 3:12–17

[God] has said, 'I will never leave you or forsake you.'
Hebrews 13:5 (NRSV)

My friend told me that some recent repair work in her block of flats required that the electricians turn off the power. She said that she quickly realised how many conveniences she took for granted. The lack of power made everyday tasks impossible: no light, no television, no washing machine, no refrigerator or freezer. She couldn't cook food or boil a kettle of water or work on the computer or listen to music. Her family's life was paralysed. When the electricity finally came back on, happiness reigned!

It seems that something similar happens in the way we regard God's gifts; we take them for granted: air, water, sunlight, the changing of the seasons, birdsong, flowers, food, a roof over our heads, health, a good mood. How often we delight in all these and more—forgetting to thank God, who sends us these blessings. May an unending hymn of praise sound in our hearts to God—the giver of all good things!

Prayer: *Dear God, your love for us is made clear in all your gifts to us, especially the gift of your Son. Thank you for your endless grace. Amen*

Thought for the day: Today I will pay more attention to God's gifts of life and love.

Irina Ivanova (Pskov, Russia)

Weakness=Strength?

Read 2 Corinthians 12:7–10

For Christ's sake, I delight in weaknesses, in insults, in hardships, in persecutions, in difficulties. For when I am weak, then I am strong.
2 Corinthians 12:10 (NIV)

In job interviews, I am always asked to describe my strengths. One day while preparing for an interview I realised that the more appropriate request would be for me to describe my weaknesses. As a Christian, I am stronger when I am at my weakest and lowest point because Christ strengthens me. At these times I am more willing to submit to his will rather than relying on my strength or knowledge.

I have learned that I can view these times as opportunities to identify and face my weakness so that Christ can strengthen me. When my self-esteem is low, I may be tempted to tear down others so as to hide my own insecurities. Instead I can remember Christ's love, which changes my mindset so that I no longer feel insecure. If I am feeling hatred or anger, then instead of acting on the anger, I can open my heart to Christ's unconditional love that replaces the hatred and bitterness. This applies to any emotion that we experience as weakness—including anxiety, fearfulness or frustration.

Paul's teaching in this passage may seem counterintuitive—that we are strongest when we are weak—but it's true. We have no strength in our own might or knowledge. But when we surrender our problems to Christ and place our trust in him, he will strengthen us.

Prayer: *Dear Lord Jesus, we place our trust in you so that you can replace our weakness with your strength. Amen*

Thought for the day: With Christ I can be strongest when I am weakest.

William Peoples (California, US)

Twice Over

Read Zechariah 9:9–12

The Lord says, 'Today I declare that I will restore to you double.'
Zechariah 9:12 (NRSV)

I took my young nephew Mark to a homemade ice cream shop located next to a dairy farm. He ordered a single-scoop chocolate ice cream cone. We walked outside to enjoy our treats and watch the cows grazing nearby. Distracted by the animals, Mark tipped his cone and the ice cream plopped to the ground. I watched his heart-broken face as the chocolate melted into the grass.

We hurried back to the ice cream shop to buy another cone, but the owner refused our money. Instead he freely gave us a replacement cone with a double scoop—one chocolate and one strawberry. He gave Mark twice over what he had lost.

Meditating on today's reading, I realised that God often treats us like that generous man. We hurry to God with our broken dreams, dissolved relationships and shattered hopes. Placing our hurts into his hands, we then can stay close to him through prayer and scripture. As we do, we believe that he will replace the losses in our lives with rich blessings. A settling peace, deep joy and renewed confidence will become ours—gifts from a loving and generous God.

Prayer: *O God, help us to trust you for blessings that outweigh our losses. Amen*

Thought for the day: God can give us back life we thought we had lost.

Marion Speicher Brown (Florida, US)

King without a Crown

Read Philippians 2:1–11

Blessed is the king who comes in the name of the Lord! Peace in heaven and glory in the highest.
Luke 19:38 (NIV)

Many years ago a lovely woman named Hazel from Sri Lanka stayed in our home for several weeks during a large, international church conference. During the opening worship service the king of Norway made an appearance, and when he arrived the whole congregation of 2,000 people rose and saluted him, as is our custom. King Olav was a rather modest man and wore his usual, plain grey suit.

Arriving home that night, Hazel was very quiet. When my mother mentioned how nice it had been to have the king at worship, Hazel answered, 'Yes, everything was very fine; but I had expected him to wear his crown.'

When Jesus approached Jerusalem on Palm Sunday, he wore no crown, even though the people saluted him: 'Blessed is the king who comes in the name of the Lord!'

The King of kings, Jesus, does not need a crown to be recognised. When he lived in our world, he walked with, talked with, and touched ordinary people. He was one of them. Jesus is still close to us, offering loving companionship to anyone who seeks him, teaching us to be humble servants.

Prayer: *Dear Jesus, thank you for being close to us. We are grateful that you came not as a conquering king but as a humble servant. Amen*

Thought for the day: Today I will try to be humble like Jesus.

Oystein Brinch (Oslo, Norway)

Prayer and Conflict

Read Matthew 5:43–46

Jesus said, 'You have heard that it was said, "You shall love your neighbour and hate your enemy." But I say to you, Love your enemies and pray for those who persecute you.'

Matthew 5:43–44 (NRSV)

Although I had been a schoolteacher at a rural school for a long time, one day I found myself in a predicament. Some members of staff thought that the school was right to fire one of the teachers, but others, like me, felt he shouldn't have been let go. Battle lines were drawn, and people on both sides were on edge. Many people stopped talking to their old friends. I dreaded going to work.

Then I began to read the Bible more and realised that God didn't want us to take sides and to be angry with each other. When I prayed that both groups would be reconciled, I was amazed how my feelings changed. Over a period of time, I found that I couldn't remain angry with someone I was praying for. So I prayed for all involved, especially those with whom I differed. My concern spilled over until I wanted only the best for them.

As I continued to pray for the welfare of everybody involved, my tense feelings disappeared and peace came into my heart. Soon my old friendships were alive once more.

Prayer: *Dear Lord, help us not get so caught up in differences of opinion that we forget to care for everybody involved. Help us remember we are sisters and brothers, children of your family. Amen*

Thought for the day: Prayer can restore broken friendships.

Barbara Barton (Texas, US)

Supporting Roles

Read Psalm 8:1–9

When I look at your heavens, the work of your fingers, the moon and the stars that you have established; what are human beings that you are mindful of them, mortals that you care for them?
Psalm 8:3–4 (NRSV)

During my first year at college I got my very first part in a play. I played a paperboy, and I think it was the smallest part. I came on stage, annoyed all the other characters, and left. Today, almost 30 years later, I can barely remember the plot of that play. But if anyone had asked at the time, I would have told them that it was all about the life of a paperboy—even though I was on the stage a grand total of three minutes!

I must confess that sometimes I think life is all about me—my own troubles, agendas and aspirations. However, now and then the facts bring me back to reality. I read recently that scientists estimate that over 100 billion people have lived on the earth, and that there are hundreds of millions of galaxies in the universe. All of this is in the hands of our mighty God. Even knowing this, I am still tempted to see myself as the 'star of the show'. We are told that God loves each one of us—that he has counted the number of hairs on our individual heads (see Matthew 10:30 and Luke 12:7). I find that God often reminds me that I am called to a supporting role, and that real joy is found in putting him and my neighbour first.

Prayer: *Dear God, we confess that sometimes we are wrapped up in ourselves and forget about others. Help us to open our hearts to a bigger world and a bigger love. Amen*

Thought for the day: Today, I will take a lesser role and put God and others first.

Michael Raypholtz (Ohio, US)

The Monster in the Cellar

Read Judges 6:12–24

The Lord said to [Gideon], 'Peace! Do not be afraid. You are not going to die.'

Judges 6:23 (NIV)

When I was young, I was often afraid. I dreaded dinnertime, when my mother sent me to the cellar to get a tin of vegetables. I was certain that a monster lurked there in the dark. Down the wobbly staircase I went, eyes wide, to find a tin of peas or sweet corn. Then I turned my back on the darkness, sure the monster would emerge to chase me up the stairs.

On the third step, I swallowed hard. Halfway up, my heart began to thump. At the tenth step, I couldn't breathe. Finally, I dashed into the lighted kitchen, slammed the door behind me and collapsed with relief, having escaped the monster once again. 'For goodness sake, Lori Ann!' Mother rolled her eyes, exasperated with my drama, and then she heartlessly sent me back for something else.

Fear is a powerful emotion that affects heart rates, thoughts and actions. Even as adults, we struggle against fears as big as death, as small as spiders or snakes, and as common as looking foolish. God reminds us that we have the responsibility and power not to be paralysed by fear. If we focus our thoughts on him, not on the monsters we imagine are stalking us, then like Gideon, we will find peace even in the midst of the battle.

Prayer: *Dear Father, help us to focus our thoughts on Jesus so that we remain in control of our fears. Amen*

Thought for the day: With God's help, we can manage our fears.

Lori Stanley Roeleveld (Rhode Island, US)

Desert Places

Read Philippians 4:10–14

Though the fig tree does not blossom, and no fruit is on the vines; though the produce of the olive fails, and the fields yield no food; though the flock is cut off from the fold, and there is no herd in the stalls, yet I will rejoice in the Lord.
Habakkuk 3:17–18 (NRSV)

Can anything bear fruit in the desert? I believe people of faith can answer with a resounding 'Yes!'

I am learning to put into practice principles that I have read and heard about for a long time. Even in great financial stress and crisis, we should continue to tithe and to help those in need. I am fascinated by Jesus' story of the poor widow who offered all she had to the temple treasury and received praise from Jesus (see Mark 12:41–44). It is difficult at times for us to give. When our resources diminish, so does our generosity. But this story of the widow's offering acknowledges that no matter what our circumstances are, we have something to give.

In the desert places of life, I have learned to be more grateful. I have found God's peace in spite of the conditions or circumstances of my life. And in doing so, I have been able to offer encouragement to others. I have also found my own faith renewed.

Prayer: *Dear loving God, in our desert places you fill us with hope. We thank you and trust you in all the circumstances of our lives. Amen*

Thought for the day: God always provides streams of water for our journey through the desert (see Isaiah 35:6).

Narda Guerrero (Dominican Republic)

Stronger than we can imagine

Read Amos 4:13 and 5:8

The people living in darkness have seen a great light; on those living in the land of the shadow of death a light has dawned.
Matthew 4:16 (NIV)

God is vaster, stronger than we can imagine; the towering mountains and crashing waves of the sea that break over the shore are details to him. He can increase the wind or fling stars into the dark; he can turn the very mountains to dust, the dawn into day and back again into night.

I love to sit by the sea and hear the billows, to stride over the mountains and smell the scent of heather, to taste the cool air. I love to watch the coming of night, and then to stir to life again in the grey morning. Each of these experiences tells me of God's all-embracing care, the rhythm of nature he created, the greatness of life itself. His light enlarges my mind, his plenty stirs my heart. And there is the special central joy that he reveals his purposes of love to us human beings. His winds refresh me; his footprints shape my life. His designs are grand, yet he cares generously and tenderly for us. He is in the heights and the depths. He is present everywhere, even though I do not see him. The hope of the return of daylight after the night is a certain illustration: the darkness is only temporary.

Prayer: *God who made the mountains, the stars and the surging seas, teach me to discern your presence in the world's rhythms—and in my own. Amen*

Thought for the day: Let us approach each new day and chapter of life with God, our Lord and Redeemer.

Rosey Feuell (Cambridgeshire, UK)

Righteousness

Read Hebrews 10:16–22

[God's] righteousness is given through faith in Jesus Christ to all who believe.
Romans 3:22 (NIV)

Because I don't do much baking, I haven't invested in many utensils and often have to improvise. For instance, when following directions that call for 'a large mixing bowl', I can compare only among the dishes I own myself, hoping they will be the right size. Unfortunately, this sometimes results in overflowing batter when, in fact, my largest bowl is too small.

Personal righteousness is similar. We compare ourselves to things most familiar to us—other people. We may think that as we haven't committed adultery or murdered anyone, and because we are honest, unlike some, surely God is pleased with us.

Scripture tells a different story. God doesn't compare us to our neighbours or even to the likes of Christian martyrs. The measure of righteousness is God's own perfection. When called 'Good Teacher', Jesus answered, 'No one is good but God alone' (Mark 10:18, NRSV). Compared to this standard, we all fall woefully short. Thankfully, our compassionate God 'made [Christ] to be sin who knew no sin, so that in him we might become the righteousness of God' (2 Corinthians 5:21). Through Christ we can approach God in confidence, knowing that instead of our sinfulness, God sees the righteousness of Jesus Christ in us.

Prayer: *Dear Father, thank you for making a provision for us through the sacrifice of your Son. Amen*

Thought for the day: God measures us against Christ's sacrifice.

Lisa Stackpole (Wisconsin, US)

One Day at a Time

Read Matthew 6:25–34

Strive first for the kingdom of God… and all these things will be given to you as well.

Matthew 6:33 (NRSV)

Many people in our church community are without work. Most of them are struggling to make ends meet, and as result a number of churches are affected financially. Recently, there were insufficient funds in the church bank account to pay our bills and not much scope for further budget cuts. We wanted to continue our ministry of worshipping, caring and growing toward a Christ-healed Africa, but our mission needed money. I confess I was anxious.

As I was sitting at the funeral of a colleague on a Friday morning, I had the distinct sense of God encouraging me to stop fussing and fretting about the church and to get on with the work to which I have been called. God's peace enfolded me. That very Sunday, a church member handed me an envelope and explained that she had had a dream in which her late husband instructed her to give this to the church. The envelope contained enough money to wipe out our deficit and keep us going for another few months! God had provided. I know full well a church cannot rely on single gifts for daily running costs, but I thank God I have learned all over again that this is primarily his work, not mine. We are privileged to be called to play a part and to trust him one day at a time.

Prayer: *Dear giving God, this day we choose to serve you and trust you for our every need. Amen*

Thought for the day: God is in charge, so I will trust.

Jeanette Krige (Gauteng, South Africa)

Nothing Can Separate Us from God's Love

Read Psalm 34:18

I am convinced that neither death, nor life, nor angels, nor rulers, nor things present, nor things to come, nor powers, nor height, nor depth, nor anything else in all creation, will be able to separate us from the love of God in Christ Jesus our Lord.
Romans 8:38–39 (NRSV)

Over a year later, we still can't believe it. I remember the phone call from my wife's middle sister when their older sister passed away. Another call, later in the evening, explained that their sister had taken her own life. My wife was devastated.

None of us had seen her sister's suicide coming, and all of us wondered why. While I can speculate and offer opinions, I probably will never understand why the tragedy occurred.

The outpouring of love from family, friends, neighbours and church members helped my wife through those challenging days. Friends had the courage to tell her their stories of losing loved ones in similar ways.

Even though suicide creates a sad and unexplainable void in many lives, I am certain that as Romans 8:38–39 assures us, nothing can separate us from the love of God.

Prayer: *Dear heavenly Lord, when our hearts are broken in tragedy, help us to feel your love. Amen*

Thought for the day: Even in tragic times, we can bear God's light to others.

Bill Pike (Virginia, US)

PRAYER FOCUS: FAMILIES DEALING WITH SUICIDE

More Fruit

Read Galatians 5:17–26

In days to come Jacob will take root, Israel will bud and blossom and fill all the world with fruit.
Isaiah 27:6 (NIV)

When spring arrives, I can smell my rosemary bush before I see it. Healthy rosemary plants can produce masses of fragrant leaves and tiny purple blossoms; fruitful growth is part of the plant's DNA.

Blooming plants like these remind us that fruitful abundance is also God's plan for humans, both the Israelites of the old covenant and Christ's followers. Just as healthy trees produce a wealth of apples or apricots, healthy Christians yield a profusion of love, joy and peace. God didn't design us to live a stingy existence with only enough compassion and patience for a few people. God wants the abundance of our spiritual fruit—the love, joy and patience that reflect God's image in us—to fill our homes and communities with the fragrance of Christ.

Picture a single fruit, and then imagine more of it. More strawberries. More peaches. More fresh melons. If there's more fruit on the plant, isn't there more for everyone to enjoy? That's the reward of abundance, both for plants and trees and for God's children.

Prayer: *Dear Lord, we open our hearts to you as the source of spiritual life. Tend our hearts until they overflow with the fruit of your love. Amen*

Thought for the day: God designed us for fruitfulness.

Donna Savage (Nevada, US)

Remembering

Read Exodus 12:14–19

[Jesus] took bread, gave thanks and broke it, and gave it to them, saying, 'This is my body given for you; do this in remembrance of me.'
Luke 22:19 (NIV)

Many years ago, when we got married, we had the wedding ceremony and evening reception videoed; recently we watched the video again. It was amazing how many details we had forgotten even though we had often talked about the wedding over the years.

Throughout the Bible God tells people to do things so that future generations will remember important events. He instituted the Passover meal to remind the Israelites of their release from Egypt. Offering sacrifices reminded the Hebrew people of their sins and the forgiveness that they could have.

Jesus commanded his disciples to remember his death and sacrifice by observing the Last Supper. The early disciples celebrated this meal regularly. No doubt they focused on how the events affected their lives and recalled the words Jesus had spoken while he was with them.

How important it is that, in addition to remembering the everyday events of our lives, we also take time to remember and tell others what God has done for us.

Prayer: *Dear God of past, present and future, we thank you for all that you have done for us, and we ask that you help us always to remember your goodness and love. Amen*

Thought for the day: Today I will remember the good things God has done for me.

Mark A. Wallace (Suffolk, England)

Everyday Mission Work

Read John 15:12–17

Jesus said, 'This is my commandment, that you love one another as I have loved you.'
John 15:12 (NIV)

Over the past year, my mother's health problems required an inordinate amount of time in hospitals and doctors' surgeries. Even though her energy was very low, her illness gave her the opportunity to reach out to those who needed compassion. A grumpy nurse and several individuals who live alone are just a few who were uplifted by her friendliness during uncomfortable medical treatments and by the daily phone calls she made from her bed. Mum did what Jesus would do: she reached out to others when she herself was experiencing a major challenge.

During this same time, my dad stepped up and changed his usual routine in order to take superb care of my mother. By making sure she rested, fielding her phone calls and assuming all household chores, he not only helped her face her health problems, but also conserved some of her energy so she could still tend to others. They both adjusted their daily routine to continue to serve others, both in and out of the home. Small, quiet, everyday missions like these are probably common, but they often go unnoticed. We can share Jesus' compassion by serving others in the midst of difficult times.

Prayer: *Dear God, help us to remember to show your love to others, especially when we ourselves are suffering. Amen*

Thought for the day: Reaching out to others with the love of Christ refocuses our challenges.

Brenda Motter (Florida, US)

Free to All

Read Romans 10:10–17
How are they to proclaim [the Lord] unless they are sent? As it is written, 'How beautiful are the feet of those who bring good news!' But not all have obeyed the good news.
Romans 10:15–16 (NRSV)

I waited anxiously at the registration desk. It was 30 minutes past the scheduled starting time yet only three participants had arrived. The organisation had brought in the best instructor and organised every detail of the professional training. All the students had to do was come and learn; no payment was required. 'Why don't they come?' I thought. This was a disaster.

Later that night as I lay in bed exhausted, I prayed: 'Lord, help me not to give in to discouragement. Please bring more participants tomorrow because this course could help them so much with their careers. Amen.' On Sunday the course ended with over half of the expected number.

This experience reminds me of an event infinitely greater than this professional training session. At Calvary God gave us the precious gift of salvation. Jesus stands with open arms and bids us to come to him and receive everlasting life at absolutely no cost. Many have accepted this gift, yet many more have not. As workers in God's vineyard, we can pray for the many who have not accepted the gift of salvation, and we can act as his hands and feet to spread the message to everyone we meet.

Prayer: *Dear God, give your children a heart of compassion and tenacity to carry your gift of salvation to unbelievers. Prepare their hearts to welcome your Son. Amen*

Thought for the day: Every day I can be available to tell the good news of Christ.

Frankie Kapendo (Addis Ababa, Ethiopia)

When It's Hard to Praise

Read Psalm 145:1–7

My heart overflows with a goodly theme; I address my verses to the king; my tongue is like the pen of a ready scribe.
Psalm 45:1 (NRSV)

From a writer's perspective, nothing is more daunting than a blank page. When I open a new document on my computer, I know that I have to fill that page—and many more—with words. Getting started is often the hardest part.

Tentatively at first, I write one word and then another and another. Once I have written those first words, more usually follow. They may not be the best I could choose, but at least they are words. I keep writing—sentence after sentence, revision after revision—until I have created something worth reading.

Sometimes praising God is just as difficult for me as putting words on paper. I feel as though I have nothing to say to the Holy One. But if I am willing to utter a few tentative words of thanks and praise, then the Holy Spirit comes to my rescue. My heart soon overflows with a goodly theme: the grace and mercy and love of God revealed in Jesus Christ.

Prayer: *Thank you, Holy Spirit, for helping us to praise God. Amen*

Thought for the day: The cure for 'praiser's' block is to start praising.

Mark M. Redfearn (California, US)

Learning to Fly!

Read Ephesians 4:1–8

There is one body and one Spirit… one God and Father of all, who is above all and through all and in all.

Ephesians 4:4–6 (NRSV)

Every year, my husband and I watch house martins nest in our garden. We enjoy watching the parents busily feed their new babies. One evening, a flock of them was flying all around the garden, crying out excitedly. The adult birds were flying with a small baby bird in their midst! Some would fly above and in front of the baby urging the baby on while the others would fly behind and below. I soon realised I was witnessing a baby martin learning to fly! The baby bird had emerged from life in a dark nest and, with the help of the flock, was flying into a bright, beautiful and new world. The whole flock seemed to be dancing in the sky and was celebrating the event with joy.

New Christians emerge from the darkness of unbelief into a new life of faith in the body of Christ. Brothers and sisters in the faith can become like that flock of birds, lifting new Christians up, urging them on and encouraging them in the faith. We can celebrate their faith journey with joy because we know these new Christians will experience a relationship with God and feel his limitless love.

Prayer: *Dear God, inspire us through the help of your Holy Spirit to encourage our brothers and sisters in the faith as we celebrate with joy our relationship with you. Amen*

Thought for the day: How can I help new Christians in their faith journey?

Ramona Barr (Texas, US)

A Humble Prayer

Read Luke 18:9–14

The prayer of the righteous person is powerful in what it can achieve.
James 5:16 (CEB)

Before retiring, I served on the pastoral staff of Sydney's Wesley Mission. It is centrally located on one of the city's main streets, not far from two underground railway stations and several city bus routes. Many people with special needs meet at the mission and find it to be a place of care. In one of several congregations for which I was responsible, almost half of the members were living with mental illness, a number of them with schizophrenia.

After one of our weekly lunch-hour services, I saw two men patiently waiting for me in the glass-walled church. I went over and sat with them.

'We would like you to pray with us,' they said.

As soon as I had prayed, one of the men prayed, 'God, save us from doing anything to harm ourselves or anyone else.'

Twelve years later, I am still deeply moved by his prayer. I am blessed by his deep cry for God's help and by the prayer's sincerity, simplicity, humility and trust.

Prayer: *O God, move us all with a deeper caring for people who are living with mental illness. May our actions reflect our concern and our lives reflect your love. Amen*

Thought for the day: The prayers of humble people have the power to change us.

Bruce Noble (New South Wales, Australia)

With Whom Are You Walking?

Read Micah 6:6–8

What does the Lord require of you? To act justly and to love mercy and to walk humbly with your God.

Micah 6:8 (NIV)

These words from the prophet Micah serve as a reminder of what God requires of us. First, God wants us to do what is right—obeying both his laws and the laws of the land in which we live. Second, he requires that we love mercy, having compassion on others without judging them or their situation. Third, we are to walk humbly with him—putting our will aside and allowing him to lead the way.

In the book of Genesis, we learn that we were created in God's image. I often ask myself, 'Am I reflecting God's image today?' The words of Micah above are the gauge I use to monitor my actions. When I am in a position of authority, do I do what is right? If others offend me, do I forgive or hold on to the pain and wait for an opportunity to hurt them in return? Am I humble in my walk with God, allowing him to lead my steps, or do I rely on only my qualifications and contacts?

Jesus sums up Micah's message when he says that we are to love the Lord our God with all our hearts, all our souls and all our minds, and love our neighbours as ourselves (see Matthew 22:34–40).

Prayer: *Dear heavenly Father, lead us today as we try to walk humbly with you. Help us to see you in everyone we meet so that we may show your mercy and your righteousness to them. Amen*

Thought for the day: How well does my life reflect the image of God?

Antoinette Knights (New York, US)

Facing Financial Fears

Read James 2:14–17

God will meet all your needs according to the riches of his glory in Christ Jesus.

Philippians 4:19 (NIV)

I was sitting at the table with Mary and two other women from church. We had recently started meeting for a weekly Bible study. Mary suddenly started sobbing. 'We don't have enough money to pay this month's bills. I don't know what we're going to do.'

'God will supply all your needs,' I quickly said, paraphrasing Philippians 4:19. I was a new Christian, and I felt confident that Mary would be comforted by this verse and assured to know she did not have to worry about her financial problems.

It wasn't until years later when my own family was short of money that I realised how flippant I must have sounded to Mary that day. My husband Kurt was recovering from brain surgery and unable to work, and bills were an added burden. No one merely recited a Bible verse to us. Instead, loving, generous friends and members of the church fulfilled the scripture by bringing us meals and giving us supermarket gift vouchers. God works through us to do his will on earth.

Prayer: *Thank you, dear God, for the generous people who help us when we are in financial need. Open our eyes to see those who need our help. As Jesus taught us, we pray, 'Father, hallowed be your name, your kingdom come. Give us each day our daily bread. Forgive us our sins, for we also forgive everyone who sins against us. And lead us not into temptation.'* Amen*

Thought for the day: In what tangible ways can I help someone today?

Sue Carloni (Wisconsin, US)

At Home with the Lord

Read John 14:1–6

Precious in the sight of the Lord is the death of his faithful ones.
Psalm 116:15 (NRSV)

I am writing this on what would have been my brother John's 66th birthday.

He was born with severe physical handicaps; he had a good mind but it was trapped in a very limited body. He could not walk, dress or feed himself or talk properly. But he loved God and was an active member of his church as far as he was able.

After the death of his parents he came to live in residential care near me. His main concern was to have someone read the Bible for him every day, and one of the other residents took on this task, reading *The Upper Room* devotionals and associated Bible passages.

As John became frailer this was his spiritual life, and he longed for the day when God would say to him, 'Come home.' Finally that day arrived and John just closed his eyes and went to glory.

Yes, I miss him, as do those who cared for him, but for John, he is 'at home', safe with the Lord he loved.

Prayer: *Thank you, Lord, for all those who witness to you despite the problems in their lives. Amen*

Thought for the day: Those we love who have died are safe with the Lord.

Hilary Hartley (East Sussex, England)

God is Light

Read 1 John 1:1–10
God is light; in him there is no darkness at all.
1 John 1:5 (NIV)

As I take my morning walk, I am surrounded by God's beautiful handiwork: an uninterrupted blanket of wild flowers; thousands of small yellow butterflies fluttering from flower to flower; the aroma of wild mint and clover. I hear the songs of birds as they sing to their mates, build nests and gather seeds and insects for their young. The sun is not quite up, but the sky is already turning a deep, cloudless blue.

Most days I am only slightly aware of the beauty of God's creation. Depression has clouded my mind and will not let go of me. This illness is devastating. Even though God has blessed me in all areas of my life, I have had a feeling of darkness and impending doom for most of my 62 years.

God's word has been my source of help. There is no darkness in him. Just because darkness fills my mind, my heart does not feel hopeless. Jesus is alive and well in my heart. God shines a light on my inner being that no darkness can overcome. 'The Lord is my light and my salvation—whom shall I fear?' (Psalm 27:1, NIV). Depression may not leave during my lifetime, but I can be confident that my Lord and Saviour is always with me to comfort me and to give me hope.

Prayer: *Thank you, dear God, for being the light that overcomes darkness. Thank you for your peace and hope. Amen*

Thought for the day: Jesus walks with us through all hardships.

Robert M. White (Texas, US)

Simple Tasks

Read 1 Corinthians 4:8–13

We are hungry and thirsty, we are poorly clothed and beaten and homeless and we grow weary from the work of our own hands… We have become like the rubbish of the world.

1 Corinthians 4:11–13 (NRSV)

Sometimes, I am amazed how the simplest task is rewarded. Even our cast-offs may be a source of inspiration for other people. One morning, I took used copies of *The Upper Room* and some religious pamphlets to a local mission. The devotional booklets were placed on a table to be available for the people who came to a chapel service before lunch.

As I waited for the doors to open, I glanced at the homeless women and men who waited with me and wondered if any of them would read the devotions in search of faith for their challenging circumstances. Would they share the booklets with others in our city who lived on the streets?

Later that afternoon, I received a call from the chaplain. 'All the materials you brought were gone in a matter of minutes. Thank you so much,' he exclaimed.

God recycles our meagre offerings into something new, often in ways and places we could never imagine.

Prayer: *Dear eternal God, thank you for opportunities to serve our neighbours. Help us to spread your love and your words to the people we meet this day. Amen*

Thought for the day: How can my recycling efforts be life-giving?

Emily Tipton Williams (Texas, US)

Agents of God's Reign

Read Acts 1:6–11

Jesus said, 'You will receive power when the Holy Spirit has come upon you; and you will be my witnesses… to the ends of the earth.'

Acts 1:8 (NRSV)

In our reading from Acts, Jesus was reiterating what he had said before: 'About that day and hour no one knows, neither the angels of heaven, nor the Son, but only the Father' (Matthew 24:36, NIV). Jesus' parables consistently conclude with the challenge for his followers to be 'faithful servants' who are doing their Lord's work every day with the urgency of those who know that any day could be their last.

The good news is that we are given power to live now in ways that are consistent with the values of God's kingdom. We are called to prepare the way for God's reign of gracious love, social justice, human reconciliation and peace in our world.

God's promise is not to destroy this world but to redeem it: 'God did not send the Son into the world to condemn the world, but in order that the world might be saved through him' (John 3:17, NRSV). With these words Jesus calls us not to abandon this earth but to be a part of its healing and redemption by the power of the Spirit of God at work in us.

Prayer: *Dear God, bring healing to the world through our witness. Amen*

Thought for the day: How will I prepare the way for God's kingdom on earth?

James Harnish (Florida, US)

Guided by the Spirit

Read Romans 8:22–27

The Spirit helps us in our weakness; for we do not know how to pray as we ought, but that very Spirit intercedes with sighs too deep for words.
Romans 8:26 (NRSV)

Our village in Eastern Democratic Republic of the Congo lies in a mountainous region of equatorial tropical forest. There is a story about a seven-year-old boy who was sent by his parents to the nearest village to look for firewood. On his way, he met a lion. Frightened, he stopped and couldn't move. However, the young boy remembered the prayer he had been taught by his parents; he closed his eyes and prayed like this, 'O Lord, bless this food before we eat it. In Jesus name, Amen.' Miraculously, when he opened his eyes, he could not see the lion, and he continued on his way.

His short prayer, uttered out of context, was nonetheless answered. His prayer was no better than anyone else's. For each of us the Holy Spirit intercedes and shapes our prayers. Prayer does not depend on particular words or repetitive sentences. Prayer is guided by the Holy Spirit. How many times have we found ourselves praying for things other than the ones we intended? That is the Spirit working through our prayers. None of us knows how to pray without the help of the Holy Spirit.

Prayer: *Dear Lord, let your Holy Spirit lead our prayers, and teach us to pray every day. Amen*

Thought for the day: Our prayers are shaped and made powerful by the Holy Spirit.

Milly Ibanda (North Kivu, Democratic Republic of Congo)

Hope and a Future

Read Jeremiah 29:11–13
'I know the plans I have for you,' declares the Lord, 'plans… to give you hope and a future.'
Jeremiah 29:11 (NIV)

For many years, I worked with lost and troubled young people in a juvenile detention centre. I often prayed that I would be able to plant a seed in these young people that would eventually bear fruit in their lives. A number of years after I retired, I received a letter from a young woman with whom I had worked more than ten years before. She thanked me for caring about her at a difficult time in her life, and she wanted to let me know about her life today. She was happily married with two children, living a faith-filled Christian life, working as an advocate at an AIDS clinic and attending college.

Later we met up, and in the course of our conversation, I asked her how she had come so far when many in similar circumstances had not made positive changes in their lives. She answered simply, 'I found God.' At a turning point in her life, she had prayed for guidance and was blessed with a path when she came across this verse: 'You make known to me the path of life' (Psalm 16:11, NIV). Today, her faith, the word of God, her Christian husband and her church encourage her to lead a fruitful life.

When I met that confused young girl many years ago, only God could know that one day she would inspire me to persevere on his path.

Prayer: *Dear God, thank you for guidance when we most need it, and thank you also for the grace to follow that guidance. Amen*

Thought for the day: How can I help lead someone to God's path today?

Dorothy Haverbusch (Ohio, US)

A Charge to Keep

Read Psalm 71:14–18

Grey hair is a crown of glory; it is found on the path of righteousness.
Proverbs 16:31 (CEB)

Reaching retirement was a milestone that promised long-awaited rewards. I looked forward to travelling, indulging in long-delayed hobbies and enjoying the benefits of my retirement income. It soon became apparent, though, that a seemingly endless parade of self-indulgent activities was not a fulfilling lifestyle for me.

Something was missing, even at the end of a beautiful day of golf or sightseeing. I had an aching sense of unfulfilled need for a deeper relationship with God and my Saviour. I experienced a painful awareness that serving and giving of myself are essential priorities in the life of a Christian, at any age.

This recent reawakening drives me to seek a balance—to attend to maintaining my health, intellectual ability and social growth, and to improve my creative skills. More importantly, I continue to use my talents and resources to focus on local and global service. I now find that retirement can be a ticket to becoming more—rather than less—involved in the work of our Lord.

Prayer: *Dear Father, continue to show us where our love and work are most needed. Amen*

Thought for the day: Each season of life opens many doors for the loving Christian.

Peter A. Moore (South Carolina, US)

A Transformed Mind

Read 2 Timothy 1:1–7

God hath not given us the spirit of fear; but of power, and of love, and of a sound mind.

2 Timothy 1:7 (KJV)

Anxiety runs in my family. My mother suffered from depression and a panic disorder that made her seem distant and unaffectionate. But in the 1970s, depression was not widely understood as a disease. We simply accepted that our silent mother who cooked, cleaned and sewed for us rarely laughed or even smiled. She never complained, merely endured.

As a young adult, I was happy to break free from my gloomy home. But years later, as a mother with a successful career, I found myself falling prey to the same mental patterns. When a problem or crisis cropped up, I became tense and prone to panic. I constantly believed disaster was imminent. This build-up of tension led to a breakdown. One day I couldn't get out of bed, immobilised by fear. My doctor prescribed medication, and though it helped, I also wanted to ask for God's healing. I recognised mental habits that needed to be changed and believed in God's power to set me free.

I began to meditate on God's word. 'God has not given me a spirit of fear,' I would repeat over and over as panic welled up inside, making my heart race. Soon I would feel calm wash over me, the calm of God's power and love, and a sound mind. Years later, I can report that God did indeed give me a sound mind. I rarely experience anxiety now, but when I do, I remember this verse.

Prayer: *Dear God our Helper, thank you for delivering us from fear and bringing peace to our troubled minds and hearts. In Jesus' name. Amen*

Thought for the day: God's peace helps us face all of life's challenges.

Elizabeth Penney (Georgia, US)

Come Boldly

Read Hebrews 4:14–16

Through [Jesus] we… have access to the Father by one Spirit.
Ephesians 2:18 (NIV)

We stood in the corridor of the government offices in Cameroon, West Africa, where we were missionaries. A large notice said we could go no further without a special appointment to see the Minister of Health, and appointments were only available on certain days. We had no appointment, and it was the wrong day. But we had travelled for two days to reach the city, and we needed to see the minister that day to register our Mission Health Centre.

'Stay here and pray,' said my husband as he walked boldly through the open door of the secretary's office. He asked her in his limited French 'Is it possible to see the minister?'

At that moment, the Minister opened his door. 'Good morning,' he said in our own language. 'Can I help you?' He invited my husband into his office where they chatted like old friends. He provided us with the signed papers we needed. Sometimes it pays to be bold!

Since Jesus has opened the way for us, we can come boldly before God—no appointment necessary. Let us not hesitate but come boldly before him with our needs.

Prayer: *Dear Jesus, thank you for sacrificing so much to open the way for us. Remind us to come boldly and thankfully into your presence. Amen*

Thought for the day: When we approach, God opens the door in welcome.

Marion Turnbull (Manchester, England)

A New Tradition

Read Matthew 7:7–12

This is the day that the Lord has made; let us rejoice and be glad in it.
Psalm 118:24 (NRSV)

Shortly after returning from church, my wife and I were greeted by our children and grandchildren. On a day of warm summer breezes, bright sunshine and a few lazy clouds, we celebrated Fathers' Day. We enjoyed a beautiful day together filled with the sounds of children's laughter. What a delight to watch the family enjoy the simple pleasures that God has given us!

After everyone had gone home, I reflected on the day. I realised that over the years, I had never thought of making our heavenly Father part of our family celebration. Next year, I will suggest a new tradition—that we attend church together as part of our celebration. What a gift that would be for our Father in heaven and for our entire family!

Prayer: *Dear heavenly Father, guide us through our lives. Help us to recognise the ways you have blessed us so that we can praise you every day, as we pray, 'Our Father which art in heaven, Hallowed be thy name. Thy kingdom come. Thy will be done in earth, as it is in heaven. Give us this day our daily bread. And forgive us our debts, as we forgive our debtors. And lead us not into temptation, but deliver us from evil: For thine is the kingdom, and the power, and the glory, for ever. Amen.'**

Thought for the day: How can I invite God into my family celebrations?

Robert Beaudoin (Connecticut, US)

The Impact of a Loving Father

Read Deuteronomy 6:4–9

Recite [the words I am commanding you] to your children and talk about them when you are at home and when you are away.
Deuteronomy 6:7 (NRSV)

This Father's Day, I reflect on my dad and the blessings he has passed on to me. I remember planting the garden with him, learning to swim under his coaching, and going with him to the shops each week. In everything we did together when I was a child, I felt cherished.

Dad taught me many life lessons. One was the value of hard work. Another was honesty. If a cashier gave him too much change, even a few pennies, he would quickly return it. My dad also taught me about the importance of spending time with God. We had family prayers nearly every evening, sometimes to my protests. Dad firmly said, 'It's time for prayers', even if I was watching my favourite TV show.

As an older adult, my dad has demonstrated grace in difficult times. He has been a carer for two spouses. He has embodied love, faithfulness, sacrificial giving and strong faith.

I think about people who have no pleasant memories of a loving father, and I pray that they will discover God's love through other significant people. I am grateful to have had a dad who served as a role model and helped me to grow spiritually.

Prayer: *Dear loving God, thank you for parents who embody your grace and love. May those who grow up in homes without good parenting encounter other people who will demonstrate your love for them. Amen*

Thought for the day: Thank God for a parent's love.

Anne Trudel (Tennessee, US)

Do We Know What We're Doing?

Read Luke 6:27–36

Jesus said, 'Love your enemies, do good to those who hate you, bless those who curse you, pray for those who mistreat you.'
Luke 6:27–28 (NIV)

When I hear news of a crime, I immediately pray for the victims and their families. It is easy to pray for the victims of crime, but how can we even think about praying for the criminals?

In Luke 6:27–28, Jesus is asking us to do something that is against our basic instincts. Our human nature too often insists that we seek revenge when someone does harm to an innocent person; we demand justice or punishment. What Jesus asks of us seems to be impossible.

But God created and loves us all—even criminals. As Christians, we are instructed to love and pray for all of God's people, not just the ones whom we deem good and respectable.

After all the torture and humiliation that Jesus endured during his crucifixion, he said, 'Father, forgive them, for they do not know what they are doing' (Luke 23:34). As followers of Christ, we can embrace and follow his example, beginning with prayer.

Prayer: *Dear God of grace, teach us to forgive others as you forgive us. Amen*

Thought for the day: God loves all people and commands us to do likewise.

Jerry J. Hurt (Ohio, US)

Walking in His Light

Read John 1:1–5

Jesus spoke to them, saying, 'I am the light of the world. Whoever follows me will never walk in darkness but will have the light of life.'
John 8:12 (NRSV)

On the day we moved to our new farm home in January 1940, my eight-year-old world suddenly became larger and more intimidating than ever before. After supper, Dad invited me to go with him to check the animals for the night. As we walked, my dad's kerosene lantern swung, its light moving back and forth as though alive. The shadows seemed to move and come ever closer. 'Dad!' I cried out in fear. He suddenly stopped, and I ran smack into him. Dad's chuckle came just before he said, 'Don't be afraid. Just walk to the edge of the light.'

Just as my earthly father comforted me, so our heavenly Father comforts us in our moments of fear, when darkness threatens to consume us. As our quoted verse states, if we follow Jesus, we will never walk in darkness.

When the nightly news is filled with reports of economic stress, terrorism, catastrophic weather and uncertainty for the future of our families, darkness can overwhelm us. Yet even in the darkest moments, the light of Christ still goes before us. His light shines in the darkness and the darkness cannot overcome it. We need not fear. Christ is constantly providing a circle of his light as our place of safety and comfort.

Prayer: *Dear heavenly Father, even though the future is not clear, may we find comfort in the knowledge that you are already there, lighting the way. In Jesus' name we pray. Amen*

Thought for the day: Jesus has commissioned us to share his light with the world.

Jack D. Kendall (Iowa, US)

PRAYER FOCUS: THOSE FACING DARK DAYS

Cherishing Love

Read Psalm 119:169–176

I have gone astray like a lost sheep; seek out your servant.
Psalm 119:176 (NRSV)

I don't know how Ruby does it. Fifty-five years after she and Ted were married, Ted is now lost in dementia. Hopelessly confused about what day it is and where he is, Ted hardly knows any of their friends anymore. His behaviour is more and more problematic: he wanders off from their home on imaginary errands; he shouts at Ruby, sometimes even physically struggling with her. Yet, day in, and day out, Ruby lovingly and patiently cares for him. She accompanies him everywhere, explaining his condition to those who don't understand. Her actions are sincere; Ruby cherishes Ted. Ruby still sees, hidden behind the fog of dementia, the love of her life.

Isn't this how God loves us? Sometimes our minds are focused anywhere but on our loving Creator. At times our behaviour is so absurd that we can't even say afterwards why we did what we did. We wander like lost sheep. Yet none of it deters God; in fact, he still cherishes us. I don't know how God does it, but whenever I see Ruby, I know where she gets it from.

Prayer: *Dear Lord, you understand our weakness. When we get lost, bring our minds back to your love. Amen*

Thought for the day: We are always on God's mind.

Dorothy O'Neill (South Australia, Australia)

Blessings All Around

Read Luke 12:22–31

Seek [God's] kingdom, and these things will be given to you as well.
Luke 12:31 (NIV)

As a friend and I walked across a car park, he bent over to pick up a coin. I had walked past without seeing it, yet he acted as if he had actually been looking for it. He put the coin in his pocket and said, 'Thank you, Lord.' My friend admitted that he frequently found coins on the ground—sometimes even dollar bills. 'I look for them, so I find them,' he said. Then he added, 'It's the same with God's blessings. I look for them, and I find a lot of them!'

My friend was right. God's blessings are so abundant that we frequently take them for granted: family to care about us; friends to share laughter and tears; a home to go to, however humble it might be; talents and abilities to help us make our way in life. All these and so much more are gifts of a loving God.

After that day, I began to look for God's blessings. My friend was right; I found a lot of them! This discovery of his abiding love has helped bring contentment to my days. It has also helped strengthen my relationship with others because I realise they too are objects of his amazing love. This lesson doesn't make everyone a friend. But it does motivate me to try to treat others with the dignity and respect all God's children deserve.

Prayer: *Dear God, help us look for your presence and your blessings in all of life. Amen*

Thought for the day: God's love for us is boundless.

Gale A. Richards (Iowa, US)

He Serves, We Serve

Read Matthew 20:25–28

The Son of Man did not come to be served, but to serve, and to give his live as a ransom for many.

Matthew 20:28 (NIV)

My best friend met up with me later than I expected. 'I was washing up after the service,' she said. It didn't surprise me. She loves the Lord and loves to serve.

Washing up isn't a prerequisite to enter the kingdom of God, but serving demonstrates that we are a part of God's kingdom. Christ washed the feet of his disciples and gave himself for us. When we as Christians serve humbly—do the dirty jobs and put others first—we are being Christ's hands and feet.

When we serve, it's easier to focus on the One who called us. When we serve, we invite the Holy Spirit to use us to do great things for God's kingdom. While 'washing dishes' isn't glamorous, if we are faithful in the small, we can be entrusted with much (see Matthew 25:21).

Prayer: *Dear Lord, help us serve others as you did. Amen*

Thought for the day: How can I serve God today?

Persida Montanez (North Carolina, US)

New Strength for a New Day

Read Isaiah 43:16–21

The Lord says, 'See, I am doing a new thing! Now it springs up; do you not perceive it? I am making a way in the wilderness and streams in the wasteland.'
Isaiah 43:19 (NIV)

I was tired and moody—and in despair. I was about to sign the contract to sell our home. My dear husband of 55 years had died a few months earlier after losing his battle against cancer.

Soon after his death I realised that I could not go on living in our home with all I would have to do: maintenance, gardening in summer and snow shovelling in winter, carrying wood for the fireplaces and so on. I should have been grateful for actually finding a buyer even before the house was advertised for sale and at a time when buying and selling houses was almost impossible. But I felt bad—even a little guilty—for selling the home we had shared for all these years.

I had not had time to read I *Dag*, the Norwegian edition of *The Upper Room*, the morning before I left for the solicitors. But when I returned home, I saw the opened magazine on the kitchen table and read the words above from Isaiah 43:19. My feelings of despair eased. God did not tell me to forget my husband. He did not forbid me to think back on all the good memories with joy. Rather, he invited me to go on with my life with new strength. God is near, in both good and bad times.

Prayer: *Dear heavenly Father, we thank you for all we have received from you—especially good memories and a loving family. Amen*

Thought for the day: God helps us see a way through the wilderness.

Laila Geitz (Akershus, Norway)

The Mystery of Communion

Read Mark 14:17–25

As often as you eat this bread and drink the cup, you proclaim the Lord's death until he comes.

1 Corinthians 11:26 (NRSV)

For a long time I questioned the point of Holy Communion. Then one day it dawned on me as I walked from my pew to the altar rail. The walk was longer than I thought.

For me, Communion celebrates the long walk of Christ from life to crucifixion to resurrection. It is the walk that Christians around the world make each Communion service. It is the walk that the saints in heaven walked long before us. The bread we eat reminds me of the manna that God provided to the Israelites in the desert. The wine is the life-giving blood of God's grace that Christ gave for our salvation.

At Communion the story of our faith is constantly being retold and demanding to be heard. At Communion we are committing to serve our brothers and sisters—even the entire world. And when we glimpse the truth that lies within the mystery and Communion becomes more revelation than routine, our lives are radically transformed. Communion is a miracle that empowers and encourages us to take the love of God into the world for the sake of Christ.

Prayer: *O God, thank you for the mystery of Communion where we experience your presence. Help us to see you in those we encounter. May we know and share your love more completely. Amen*

Thought for the day: Through Communion, our lives can be radically transformed.

Patrick Christopher Kangrga (Maryland, US)

The Pepper Pot

Read Psalm 91
Whoever dwells in the shelter of the Most High will rest in the shadow of the Almighty. I will say of the Lord, 'He is my refuge and my fortress, my God, in whom I trust.'
Psalm 91:1–2 (NIV)

The southern skyline of the Isle of Wight is dominated by St Catherine's Oratory, a medieval lighthouse affectionately known by locals as the Pepper Pot. The tower was constructed by Walter de Godeton, as a penance for stealing wine from a wrecked ship that foundered off the southern coast of the island, and was completed in 1328.

One day my wife and I decided to take a walk up the steep hill to the monument. It was a wild and wintry day and the wind whipped across the desolate hillside, causing us to lean at an angle to remain upright. We could hear nothing but the roar of the wind in our ears. Having been blown and beaten on our ascent we were glad to take refuge inside the thick stone walls and were immediately struck by the calmness that welcomed us.

Life can bring us many storms. We may be facing the high winds of financial insecurity, the heavy rains of failing health or the wild gales of a relationship crisis. However, in the midst of the tempest God calls for us to find shelter in him.

By taking our problems and cares to him in prayer, we can find a peace that passes all understanding: a refuge in the storm.

Prayer: *When I feel buffeted and battered by the storms of life, help me, dear God, to know your peace and find in you a place of stillness and calm. Amen*

Thought for the day: Life has many storms. Where do I find refuge? What is my 'Pepper Pot'?

Adam Pope (Northamptonshire, England)

Carrying Baggage

Read Matthew 12:25–30

Come to me, all you who are weary and burdened, and I will give you rest.

Matthew 11:28 (NIV)

Carry-on luggage on a flight can be cumbersome. My small suitcase is swollen with personal belongings that I prefer to have within reach. I lug it on board, hoping that its girth will go unnoticed. Sometimes, my bag is too bulky to fit in the overhead luggage rack. Once, I had to take it to the front of the plane, for storage elsewhere.

As I reflected on that incident, I realised that in many ways I have treated sinful habits like carry-on luggage. I have carried around my desire for material possessions, hunger for approval and appetite for sensual pleasure. I've depended on their presence to feel good about myself. However, they offered little relief from my emotional or spiritual struggles. I am learning that God's opinion of me is what matters. And because Christ is my Lord and Saviour, I am accepted, loved and valued.

Jesus gently and lovingly calls each of us to have a personal relationship with him. When we surrender our baggage to Jesus Christ—by daily asking him to help us desire him more than our pleasures—we experience intimacy with Jesus through prayer, worship, Bible study and obedience. Jesus Christ is all we truly need. And his load—his will for our lives—is easy and light.

Prayer: *Dear Lord, thank you that we can hand our baggage over to you and experience intimacy, fellowship and rest. Amen*

Thought for the day: No pleasure can compare to relationship with Christ.

Michael Lewis (Virginia, US)

Being Accountable

Read Hebrews 10:23–25
We urge you, beloved, to admonish the idlers, encourage the fainthearted, help the weak, be patient with all of them.
1 Thessalonians 5:14 (NRSV)

I went mountain climbing the other day and met up with some energetic students. When I thought I could not possibly go on, they shouted words of encouragement: 'You can do it!' 'This is nothing. You've made it this far; the worst is over.' At times, they burst into song to boost morale. Together, we made it all the way.

This experience reminds me of our Christian walk. Sometimes the battle is too fierce, and we feel we can't go on. We don't have the strength even to pray. In such times, we need other people to support, encourage and admonish us in love. Through Christian fellowship, we have the strength to hold on to God's sure promises and to continue. Being accountable to one another keeps us on track.

Some people say that they need not go to church anymore because they listen to sermons on TV or on the internet. This practice is no substitute for Christian fellowship. The TV won't comfort us through hard times, rejoice in our blessings or keep us accountable. Our brothers and sisters in Christ will.

Prayer: *Thank you, dear God, for the fellowship of believers. Teach us to cherish it and to play our roles in the community of faith. Amen*

Thought for the day: We are members of the body of Christ and accountable to one another.

Veronica Kamidi (Nairobi, Kenya)

In Dark Times

Read Romans 8:31–39

Jesus said, 'Remember, I am with you always, to the end of the age.'
Matthew 28:20 (NRSV)

Post Traumatic Stress Disorder (PTSD) is a condition in which a vivid life experience continues to replay in thoughts and dreams and at unexpected and unwelcome times. It often originates in a life-threatening event, but it can also affect someone whose world is shaken in a less dramatic but intensely personal way. At its worst, PTSD is paralysing and hinders daily life.

As someone who has personally struggled with PTSD I have wondered, is it selfish for a person who is battling PTSD to ask God to remove the condition? We look to the scripture for an answer. Jesus healed many people, but healing was not his main focus. His assurance to us was and is that God is a source of indescribable power and strength, that he cares for us, knows our names and surrounds us with love. God may not take away, with a single stroke, the intruding images of PTSD. Healing will come at its own pace. Until then, when the images strive to take control, we can reach out to God, who stands beside us. We can be assured that we are of inestimable worth to him and that he buoys us up with love.

Prayer: *Dear God, you are on our right, on our left, in front of us and behind us. Help us to feel your love carrying us through the dark places in our lives until light shines once more. Amen*

Thought for the day: When we are in a dark place, God is next to us and yearns to take our hand.

Don Greeley (Illinois, US)

Under His Wings

Read Psalm 91:1–6
How precious is your steadfast love, O God! All people may take refuge in the shadow of your wings.
Psalm 36:7 (NRSV)

My grandparents used to raise white leghorn chickens—fowls with snow-white feathers and vivid red combs. Sometimes, as a child, I would see a hen squat on the ground, looking as if she were resting from the heat of the day. When she finally stood up, a brood of tiny chicks would come scrambling out and take up position behind their mother. Everywhere she went, the chicks would follow and if she stopped and held out her wings, they'd scurry back under. For those chicks, the safest place to be was enfolded inside her wings.

Seeing this as a child has given me insight into a statement Jesus made. He was expressing to the multitude his grief over Jerusalem because they had rejected all the prophets God had sent them. Then, in a more tender moment, he exclaimed, 'Jerusalem, Jerusalem... How often have I desired to gather your children together as a hen gathers her brood under her wings, and you were not willing!' (Matthew 23:37).

We live in a stressful world filled with problems that can seem overwhelming. Our Lord beckons us to trust him and run for protection within his arms.

Prayer: *Dear Lord Jesus, may we learn to run to you for protection. Amen*

Thought for the day: Christ's arms of protection are available every day.

Mary Baird (Texas, US)

Gifts Great and Small

Read Mark 12:41–44

All of them [rich people] are giving out of their spare change. But [one poor widow] from her hopeless poverty has given everything she had, even what she needed to live on.

Mark 12:44 (CEB)

I was picking the last green peas of the season. The vines were tall and most contained three or four pods of up to nine peas each. As I went along I found one small plant dwarfed by the rest. On it was one pod of about five peas. As I picked it I thought that it wasn't much, but it did what it could; it gave all that it had!

Sometimes we think what someone else has to give isn't much. But we are not called to judge how much someone else gives. God calls each of us to give all we can, all we feel led to give, no matter how great, no matter how small. And we are called to give thanks for all who give, no matter how great, no matter how small the gift.

Prayer: *Dear Lord, teach us gratitude for small gifts as well as great gifts and gratitude for the giver of both great and small gifts. We pray as Jesus taught us, saying, 'Our Father in heaven, hallowed be your name, your kingdom come, your will be done, on earth as it is in heaven. Give us today our daily bread. And forgive us our debts, as we also have forgiven our debtors. And lead us not into temptation, but deliver us from the evil one.'* Amen*

Thought for the day: Today I will answer God's call to give all I am able.

John Peebles (Virginia, US)

Guess Who's Back!

Read Luke 15:11–24

The father declared, 'This son of mine was dead and has come back to life! He was lost and is found!'
Luke 15:24 (CEB)

Our daughter found a stray cat in our garden. Without asking permission, she fed him. Then the inevitable happened: Old Tom made himself at home. Soon his furry grey body and quiet purr became an important part of our lives. But he had not given up his street life; he would disappear for weeks at a time. Just when we decided he was gone for good, he would return—a torn and bloody skeleton of a cat.

The prodigal son had some of Old Tom in him. But so do we! While we enjoy the comfort of being part of God's family, our independent nature at times gets us into trouble, and we end up spiritually—and sometimes even physically—starved and wounded. No matter how many times Old Tom wandered off, it was a day for rejoicing when someone shouted, 'Guess who's back!' Someone would pour him a bowl of milk and someone else would prepare a warm bath.

Our scripture tells us that God's welcome mat is always out, no matter how many times we stray. Imagine the cheering for us from heaven when someone shouts, 'Guess who's back!'

Prayer: *Dear Lord, our wilful nature causes us to stray from your loving care. Thank you for welcoming back your foolish, straying children. Amen*

Thought for the day: When we stray, God is waiting to welcome us home.

Madeline Peterson (Nebraska, US)

Gardening

Read Psalm 104:13–23

Jesus said, 'As the Father has loved me, so have I loved you. Abide in my love.'
John 15:9 (NRSV)

Recently, I have been truly enjoying my garden. I used simply to maintain it, giving it a bit of water and mowing the grass. Lately though, I have been pruning, turning the soil, adding fertiliser and then topping it with some of my husband's lovely Lucerne mulch from our hay farm. And the results have been amazing—beautiful bulbs and flowers, flowering bushes and gorgeous roses. It looks brilliant!

Our lives are like gardens. Sometimes they need to be ploughed up or have the soil turned or have branches pruned. Even though it can be painful, it is necessary to cut away the sin in our lives to make room for new growth. We need to apply the fertiliser of God's word and the water of the Holy Spirit. When we have the basics sorted out, then on top of it all we need to apply the mulch of good fellowship, worship and prayer. All of this helps to keep our hearts and minds growing strong so that we can shine brilliantly for the Lord and work for the kingdom of God.

Prayer: *Dear God of creation, thank you that you love us as the Father has loved you. You have planted good things in us. Help us to abide in your love so that we can continue to do the things necessary to keep your work alive in us. Amen*

Thought for the day: How am I tending the good things God has planted in me?

Janine Randell (New South Wales, Australia)

Noticing

Over the years I have developed three foundational convictions about the gift of God: (1) The Holy Spirit is God's personal presence; (2) The Holy Spirit is God loving us; (3) The Holy Spirit is God's grace active in our lives. Put these three convictions together, and we can celebrate one bit of good news about God's Spirit: through the Holy Spirit, God is lovingly present and always active in our lives. But experiencing more of the Holy Spirit requires involvement. Spiritual practices make it possible for us to live more deeply in the Spirit every moment.

The Holy Spirit is at work in our lives in every encounter, in our daily work, in our communities and indeed throughout our whole universe. We experience the Holy Spirit all the time. The Spirit of God always reaches out to us with God's love and grace in moments of beauty, love, rest, joy and newness. The Holy Spirit touches us—even in our pain, disappointment, grief, struggle and loneliness. We have only to recognise and respond to this ever-present activity of the Holy Spirit.

One way to begin this practice of noticing the Holy Spirit entails setting aside a block of time to pursue the following exercise. Go back over your life and notice how the Holy Spirit has been with you over the years. Make a list of gifts of love and grace that you have received—significant moments when you have felt loved, cherished and valued. These might include a moment of human love, a moment when it felt good to be alive, a moment when it seemed as if God was using you to help someone else. Write these on a piece of paper. Finally, ask God to help you notice how the Spirit has encouraged growth in your relationship to the divine.

When I first worked through this exercise, I came to a massive realisation: the Spirit had been active in my life long before my conscious choice to become a follower of Christ. As I spent time looking back, I began to recognise that the Holy Spirit had been present throughout my life—continuously bringing God's love to me, touching my life with grace and stirring up desire for God.

Once we complete this exercise, we can further grow our capacity to notice God's Spirit by looking back over each day, trying to notice where the Spirit has touched our lives. Maybe we experienced the touch of the Spirit over a cup of coffee, some help given by a colleague, an encouraging text message, a piece of work well done or some other moment we appreciated. These moments are gifts of God's love and grace, signs of the Holy Spirit at work in our lives. Noticing them allows us to experience the Holy Spirit who was lovingly present and active in them.

By using this practice of daily review, we will fine-tune our ability to receive and acknowledge the Spirit as events occur throughout the day. We will begin to receive the Spirit in every breath we take, every bite of food we eat, every hug we receive, every person we meet. Even in difficult and painful moments we will find ourselves able to receive God's love and grace. Nothing can stop God from loving us! Is this not part of what Paul meant when he shared his conviction with his readers in Rome that nothing in all creation can separate us from the love of God in Christ Jesus our Lord?

As noticing the activity of God's Spirit becomes a natural part of your everyday life, you will open yourself to experience the Holy Spirit in the here and now, which is just how God wants it to be. After all, the Holy Spirit is the gift of God given to each one of us.

Several meditations in this issue deal with the Holy Spirit. You may wish to read the meditations on the following dates again as you reflect: May 8 and 31, June 8, 9, 19, and 20, July 3 and August 24 and 31.

Questions for Reflection

1. What are your earliest memories of God's love and grace in your life?

2. What has been your most recent experience of God's love and grace?

3. What would it mean to you if you recognised the Holy Spirit as active in these experiences of God's love and grace?

4. What practice would help you notice more often the Holy Spirit's work in your everyday life?

Trevor Hudson has been part of the Methodist movement for over 30 years, primarily serving in and around Johannesburg, South Africa. Trevor travels internationally—leading conferences, retreats and workshops. This prayer workshop was adapted from Trevor's new book, *Holy Spirit Here and Now*, published in July 2013 by Upper Room Books.

Let's Pray Now

Read Ephesians 6:17–20

The prayer of the righteous is powerful and effective.
James 5:16 (NRSV)

Our men's Bible study had just ended, and as I was heading for the door I asked Timothy to pray for a concern I had. I thought he would respond by agreeing to pray as I requested, but at a later time. To my surprise he said, 'Let's pray now.'

It's so easy to say, 'I will pray for you' and then go off into our busy day with all of life's distractions. I know at times I have forgotten or failed to follow through with my promise to pray for another's concerns.

What a privilege it is to be able to pray for others, to call on the power of God to be focused on someone's need! To go to the Lord on another's behalf is truly a blessing.

I have never forgotten that moment with Timothy. Now, when someone asks me to pray for them, I say, 'Let's pray now.'

Prayer: *All-knowing and ever-present God, thank you for the blessing of prayer and the peace we receive when we come to you in prayer. Amen*

Thought for the day: Praying for others is a privilege.

Rich Robertson (Texas, US)

Looking Beyond

Read Matthew 7:1–5

Don't judge, and you won't be judged. Don't condemn, and you won't be condemned. Forgive, and you will be forgiven.
Luke 6:37 (CEB)

I work for a father-and-son maintenance company. The father is jovial and easy-going, always ready to carry out his maintenance duties with a smile. His son is the sullen, quiet, despondent type, and I admit that I had formed an unfavourable opinion of him. One day I was in the canteen for lunch at the same time as his father. I asked how his son was doing. He said, 'Well, he's doing a bit better.' I asked, 'What do you mean by "better"?' He told me his son had lost his young wife to cancer about a year ago. They had been married only one year, and his son was having a difficult time adjusting.

The father's words made me realise how quickly and easily we can judge other people without knowing anything about them. We sometimes even pass these opinions on without an iota of information about what these people might be going through.

Everyone has a story, whether we know that story or not. Matthew 7:3 reminds me as a follower of Christ to look beyond outward appearances in my relationships with my family, my friends, and my acquaintances and to share God's love with everyone.

Prayer: *God of love, open our eyes to see beyond outward appearances to the pains and struggles of our brothers and sisters. Amen*

Thought for the day: God calls us to love, not judge.

Sandra Ramirez (Ohio, US)

Miracles are Possible

Read John 21:15–17

[Jesus] said to him, 'Simon son of John, do you love me?' Peter was hurt because Jesus asked him the third time, 'Do you love me?' He said, 'Lord, you know all things; you know that I love you.'

John 21:17 (NIV)

I have had an exciting life. As a rubber planter in Malaysia I was saved from a bandit ambush and four times from deadly snakes. I survived a deep depression, brain surgery and much more. God has given me the joy of preaching and the joy of witnessing through writing books. I have seen a Christian youth group in Malaysia grow from 30 members to over 10,000 members and spread to four more countries.

Some people do not believe in miracles, but I have experienced them! All who believe Jesus is the Son of God know how he suffered and died on the cross to show God's love for us. Jesus is the Saviour. We know that Jesus is always with us through the Holy Spirit, who dwells within us. Enthusiasm to serve Jesus brings wonderful happenings, and each day can be a holy adventure.

Prayer: *Dear Jesus, thank you for being with us and for all you have done for us. Help us to serve you each day as we pray, 'Our Father in heaven, hallowed be your name, your kingdom come, your will be done, on earth as it is in heaven. Give us today our daily bread. And forgive us our debts, as we also have forgiven our debtors. And lead us not into temptation, but deliver us from the evil one.'* Amen*

Thought for the day: When we believe in Jesus, miracles are possible.

Paul Juby (Norfolk, England)

* Matthew 6:9–13 (NIV)

For Jesus

Read Matthew 25:31–40

The King will reply, '… whatever you did for one of the least of these brothers and sisters of mine, you did for me.'
Matthew 25:40 (NIV)

My 21-year-old grandson was leaving a shop with a bag of apples when he noticed a woman and her two young children outside. Warren walked up to them and handed each of the children an apple. He learned that one of the children was ill, and that even though the woman had a prescription for medicine, she did not know how to fill it. Nor did she have the money she needed.

Moved with compassion, Warren helped the woman and her children to get the medicine they needed, and also bought them some food. Then he drove them to their home. The woman was overjoyed at this act of kindness from a stranger.

In Jesus' story, the king said, 'Whatever you did for one of the least of these brothers and sisters of mine, you did for me' (Matthew 25:40, NIV). Each of us has countless opportunities to say a kind word, give a smile or do a thoughtful deed. When we take advantage of these opportunities as Warren did that morning, we encourage and spread God's love to others.

Prayer: *Dear Lord, help us to be alert for opportunities to show you that we love you by caring for others. Amen*

Thought for the day: Where will I meet Jesus today?

Sandra Hastings (Ohio, US)

The Gift of Forgiveness

Read Ephesians 1:3–10

As far as the east is from the west, so far has [God] removed our transgressions from us.
Psalm 103:12 (NIV)

Recently I lost quite a huge sum of money to a con artist who pretended to be a Christian. I was deeply hurt, and I went through the various stages of grief to get over my profound loss. What surprised me was how difficult it was for me to forgive myself for failing to ask for God's direction when investing my money. I had been a poor steward of the gifts he had blessed me with. But I realised that in order for me to accept God's forgiveness, I had to forgive myself and realise that he still loves me!

A gift is beneficial only when it is accepted, and God is willing to draw us to himself. He is gracious, compassionate, slow to anger and abounding in love. He forgives us when we fall into sin if we sincerely repent. Psalm 51:17 says, 'A broken spirit; a broken and contrite heart, O God, you will not despise.'

When I let go of my guilt and let God work in my life, revealing that divine love for me, I felt an overwhelming sense of his presence. After all, God loves me not because I do good things but because I am his child, someone for whom Christ died. And his love is for all of us.

Prayer: *O loving Father, help us to realise that you love us dearly and that your grace has no end. Amen*

Thought for the day: Forgive yourself—and allow God to work his forgiveness in your heart.

Veronica Kamidi (Nairobi, Kenya)

Part of the Whole

Read 1 Corinthians 12:12–31

You are the body of Christ and individually members of it.
1 Corinthians 12:27 (NRSV)

My cousin gave me a beautiful beaded bracelet. Her friend had designed it, and I was fascinated by each of the individual beads, which were in shades of purple, pink, blue and green. No two beads were exactly alike in colour, size or shape, and each bead made its own unique contribution; the omission of any one bead would have lessened the beauty of the bracelet.

This bracelet reminds me of Paul's description of the church being like parts of the human body. Each individual part has a specific function to perform in the body of Christ, and every part is needed and special. Paul writes that God's desire is 'that there… be no dissension within the body', so that 'the members may have the same care for one another' (1 Corinthians 12:25, NRSV). We are called to support one another and celebrate each person's role in the church.

Like the beads in my bracelet, coming together to create a beautiful whole, we in the church are called to use the unique gifts God has given us 'for the common good' (1 Corinthians 12:7, NRSV). When we come together in appreciation and support of one another's gifts, we are truly living out our role as members of the body of Christ.

Prayer: *Dear God, thank you for giving each of us a special part to play in your body. Help us to serve you faithfully each day. Amen*

Thought for the day: Each one of us is an important part of the body of Christ.

Janine Kuty (Virginia, US)

The Parquet Floor

Read 1 Corinthians 12:12–31

The one who plants and the one who waters have a common purpose, and each will receive wages according to the labour of each.

1 Corinthians 3:8 (NRSV)

All heads were bowed and all eyes closed as the group prayed for unity and co-operation. Although my head was bowed my eyes remained open as I found myself studying the floor beneath my feet.

It was wood parquet flooring, highly polished and in very good condition. I found myself marvelling at the way each piece of wood was dovetailed into the others and at the variety of shades of colour. They ranged from dark mahogany through to all tints of brown and pale cream. Studying it, I didn't look especially at one dark piece of wood or concentrate on the palest piece. The surface was smooth and pleasing to the eye. There were no pieces one could trip on.

I suddenly realised that that was exactly what we were praying for. We weren't looking for 'key players' or lowly workers, but for all to work toward the glory of God, in a united and co-operative way. Not all of us stand out in church work. Not all of us need to be in the background. God needs us all and has prepared us for tasks for him. At different times of our life we may be called upon to play different parts, but all are equally important.

Prayer: *Lord, I pray that I may do my part to fit into the plan for your kingdom. Amen*

Thought for the day: May my section of flooring not be missing.

Carol Purves (Cumbria, England)

On Eagles' Wings

Read 1 Corinthians 9:24–27

Those who hope in the Lord will renew their strength. They will soar on wings like eagles; they will run and not grow weary, they will walk and not be faint.

Isaiah 40:31 (NIV)

I walk near an eagle sanctuary as part of my daily exercise routine. One day I was tired, and I did not know if I would have the strength to walk my usual distance. I glanced upward and saw three eagles soaring above the treetops. Immediately, I remembered the scripture from that morning's meditation in *The Upper Room* (quoted above). I began to recite that scripture verse and to focus on the soaring eagles. The Lord granted me the strength to walk the entire distance that I had set as my goal for the day. As I walked, I thanked God for the natural beauty of my surroundings, especially the beauty and majesty of the eagles. I also thanked God that I had read *The Upper Room* that morning as part of my daily spiritual practice.

Many times, the demands of spiritual and physical discipline can overwhelm us, but God will answer our prayers when we ask for strength to persevere during our physical and spiritual trials. He who is everlasting and almighty is always available to help us; we only have to ask.

Prayer: *All-powerful God, please give us the strength and perseverance to live a more disciplined life. Amen*

Thought for the day: Scripture can guide and inspire us during life's trials.

Suzanne E. Wiltz (Louisiana, US)

The Other Side

Read Luke 8:22–25

One day Jesus said to his disciples, 'Let us go over to the other side of the lake.'

Luke 8:22 (NIV)

Jesus asked his disciples to 'go over to the other side' of the lake. The Sea of Galilee was subject to fierce winds and sudden violent storms that blew up without warning. Consequently, most boats would hug the shoreline so the crews could reach land quickly if a storm came up. The disciples were asked to take a risk; they were justifiably afraid. They might have refused to go. Nonetheless, they were willing to go over to the other side and get out of their comfort zone. Because they were willing to take a risk, we have this wonderful story of God's miraculous intervention.

Recently, our church was asked to take a risk and 'go over to the other side'. We were asked to be part of a city group that provided shelter for the homeless. Some in our community grumbled; some were afraid of what might happen; but we decided to try it. The storm of controversy turned into a blessing as we participated in this ministry of hospitality. Following the example of the disciples, we can have courage to 'go over to the other side' and be open to new ministries.

Prayer: *Dear Lord, we are thankful that in the midst of turmoil you have promised to be with us in the storm. Amen*

Thought for the day: How can I venture out of my comfort zone to help others in the name of Christ?

Mike Bertoglio (Washington, US)

The Power in a Name

Read John 20:11–18
Now says the Lord… Don't fear, for I have redeemed you; I have called you by name; you are mine.
Isaiah 43:1 (CEB)

'My name is John Wesley Starnes, and I am a Methodist.' I will always remember the day I met Mr Starnes as he entered the retirement home chapel. Diagnosed with Alzheimer's disease, he faithfully attended worship services for a couple of years until he became too confused. I wondered if he even knew who he was anymore. One day I saw Mr Starnes in a hallway, and I greeted him, 'Hey! Your name is John Wesley Starnes!' He rolled toward me in his wheelchair and with bright eyes and a big smile replied, 'Thank you for remembering my name and who I am.'

Jesus knows the power in a name. Upon hearing Jesus speak her name, Mary Magdalene immediately recognised him and went to tell the disciples of his resurrection. After being asked three times by his Saviour if he loved him, Simon Peter went on to build the Church (see John 21:15–19). Lazarus' sister was set free from stress and anxiety with a simple, 'Martha, Martha'.

I will always be thankful for Mr Starnes who reminded me that Jesus knows our names, who we are and what we are going through, and that he will be with us all the way to the end. I want to hear Jesus calling my name so that I might follow his will.

Prayer: *Ever-living God, give us ears to hear, hearts that discern and courage to obey your voice. Amen*

Thought for the day: Jesus is calling my name.

Bill Duckworth (Mississippi, US)

Place of Rest

Read Psalm 131:1–3

The Lord has chosen Zion, he has desired it for his dwelling, saying, 'This is my resting place forever and ever; here I will sit enthroned for I have desired it.'

Psalm 132:13–14 (NIV)

Recently, I visited a friend who lives in a flat behind a busy open market. The area is chaotic and noisy during the day, and the entrance and stairs to her home are scruffy and dingy. However, once inside her flat, I found it to be a lovely haven of rest. She has worked hard to create this sanctuary where she can pray and be at peace.

Her home environment reminds me of the contrast between the darkness, chaos and uncleanness of the world all around us and God's desire for us to be constantly at rest in the inner sanctuary of our hearts.

We too may have to work hard to replace the restless churning activity within our lives with God's presence. But we can do this by reading the Bible and listening to God's instructions. If we can persevere, we shall reap a reward and gradually come to know a stillness within that is not easily disturbed by the things around us.

Prayer: *O Lord, thank you for giving us your Holy Spirit, who dwells within us. Teach us to rest in your love. Amen*

Thought for the day: My spirit can be at peace even in the most unlikely places.

Lydia Carey (Jerusalem, Israel)

Always There

Read Genesis 12:1–7
The Lord said to Abram, 'Go from your country and your kindred and your father's house to the land that I will show you.'
Genesis 12:1 (NRSV)

I woke up one morning with a good feeling. I was simply thinking of all the ways that God has been there for me in my life. I was changing from a job that paid well to a new job where my income was much more uncertain. But instead of worrying, I felt a sense of confidence and peace.

It reminded me of the story of Abram and his obedience to the Lord. God told Abram to go to a new land that he would show him. I can't assume that Abram never wavered or doubted, but he trusted and followed God's instructions. And God was faithful and gave Abram and his descendants a new home.

God asks us to believe, to be obedient and to trust that he will always be there for us. When we face changes and times of uncertainty, we can be encouraged by the story of Abram. When we have faith and act in obedience, God will see us through. He will never fail us.

Prayer: *Dear heavenly Father, thank you for always providing for us. Even when we don't understand, help us to be obedient to your will and your way. Amen*

Thought for the day: When we put our faith and trust in God, he will always be there for us.

Byron Samuels (Florida, US)

Spiritual Water

Read John 4:1–15, 25–29

Jesus answered, 'Whoever drinks the water I give them will never thirst.'
John 4:14 (NIV)

One Saturday I drove to a nearby bakery thinking that a piece of gooey cake would soften my deep loneliness. When the shop assistant said, 'We've sold out', I left with my emotions out of control. Back at home, I realised I had tried to supply a spiritual need with a physical solution. Although I had chosen my ways over God's ways for too long, I cried out to him that night. I was amazed at how quickly I felt his presence, peace and love.

I suddenly identified with the woman in John 4. John didn't give her a name; she was just 'a Samaritan woman'. When Jesus spoke to her about living water, she said to him, 'Give me this water so that I won't get thirsty and have to keep coming here' (John 4:15, NIV). At first she didn't understand that Jesus spoke of spiritual water, but the longer he talked, the more convinced she was that he was the Messiah. Leaving her water jar, she ran to tell the people in Sychar about a man who knew all about her.

In a similar way, God's peace that Saturday night inspired me to return to a community of faithful people. I went back to church and began reading my Bible. I found the courage I needed to share with others how God had comforted me.

Prayer: *Thank you, Lord Jesus, for loving us and changing us into who you want us to be. Amen*

Thought for the day: Cake is good, but God is better.

Sue Tornai (California, US)

Where Could I Go?

Read Psalm 139:1–12

Where can I go from your Spirit? Or where can I flee from your presence?
Psalm 139:7 (NRSV)

Nestled in the Himalayas and bordered by Nepal, Tibet and China, Mount Everest is the tallest mountain in the world at 29,035 feet. Some mountain climbers have made it to the top. Other adventurers have explored earth's deepest caverns. The vast cave Krubera-Voronja is located near where Western Asia and Eastern Europe intersect. Scientists have recorded its depth at 7,188 feet.

Some places in our world, however, are still untouched by humans. But since God created our world, he is in all places on this globe and in the heavens. Why, then, do we think we can go somewhere he will not be? The psalmist realised he could not hide from God's presence. Likewise, we cannot be called by him into a circumstance or place where he doesn't precede us. What a wonderful truth to remember! After all, God said, 'I will never leave you or forsake you' (Hebrews 13:5), and Jesus reminded the disciples, 'I am with you always' (Matthew 28:20). These assurances enable us to live as faithful servants of our loving God.

Prayer: *Dear Lord, everywhere we go we see your immeasurable creativity. We pray that you will open our minds and spirits to the possibilities of what you want to do in our lives. Amen*

Thought for the day: God is with us in the heights and depths of our lives.

Peter D. Mallett (Virginia, US)

God's Open Day

Read 1 John 5:1–12

This is the testimony: God gave eternal life to us, and this life is in his Son. The one who has the Son has life. The one who doesn't have God's Son does not have life.

1 John 5:11–12 (CEB)

Recently, I attended our local high school's open day, hoping to get my son admitted for the next year. Everything was new, exciting and different, and I longed to see my son in the school. However, while 600 parents were present, the school had only 150 vacancies. I wondered if my son would get in. Then I found among the application forms a paper that stated, 'If you live in the vicinity of the school and are a rightful resident in the area, you will not be refused entry.' What a relief!

I am a relatively new Christian and often have doubts about being accepted into heaven. This experience helped me to see Easter as God's open day for entry into his heavenly kingdom. The news of the kingdom is good news for everyone. Anyone can apply. If Jesus is our Lord and Saviour and we live faithfully, our admission is guaranteed. We may fail an exam or get bad marks; but if Jesus lives in our hearts, we will get in.

Prayer: *God of all, increase our faith in your word and let us seek to live near the cross always. Amen*

Thought for the day: Because God is faithful we can be certain of eternal life.

Sue Peters (Eastern Cape, South Africa)

Live It!

Read Ezekiel 33:30–33

Do not merely listen to the word, and so deceive yourselves. Do what it says.

James 1:22 (NIV)

In the midst of busy lives, even when we make daily Bible reading a priority, we sometimes find ourselves merely scanning the pages and do not read scripture for ways that we can apply its truths. When we read the Bible as if hearing that story or that event for the first time, we can discover something new in its pages. And it can be an inexhaustible source of truth and encouragement.

The prophet Ezekiel spoke to the people of his day about applying the word of God to their lives. They loved to listen but did not do well in practising what they heard. So God spoke to Ezekiel, saying, 'To them you are like a singer of love songs, one who has a beautiful voice and plays well on an instrument; they hear what you say, but they will not do it'(Ezekiel 33:32, NRSV). Jesus expanded on this theme: 'Everyone who hears these words of mine and puts them into practice is like a wise man who built his house on the rock' (Matthew 7:24, NIV).

Scripture takes on tremendous power when we apply it every day. It addresses our problems, displaying God's concern for us and his wisdom to help solve these problems. Putting the word of God into practice can improve our relationships and give us direction for our lives. Instead of resolving only to read the Bible, we can resolve to live it!

Prayer: *Dear God, as we read your word, help us to discern your message for our lives and our hearts each day. Amen*

Thought for the day: What is God's word showing me today?

Andy Baker (Tennessee, US)

When God Takes Away

Read Job 1:13–22

[Job] said, 'Naked I came from my mother's womb, and naked shall I return there; the Lord gave, and the Lord has taken away; blessed be the name of the Lord.'

Job 1:21 (NRSV)

When we consider Job, a man who intensely loved and obeyed God and yet was stripped of his children and his vast wealth, we see his words as an astounding response to phenomenal loss.

Sometimes, people mistakenly believe that suffering is the result of wrongs committed. The disciples, for example, asked Jesus about a man born blind, 'Rabbi, who sinned, this man or his parents, that he was born blind?' (John 9:2). Yet the Bible declares that neither Job nor the blind man was afflicted because of wrongdoing. Job knew his suffering was not the result of sin. He also understood that everything he lost had been given to him by God and that whether God gives or takes away, he is worthy of praise. Why? Job trusted God in the midst of his trials, and Paul reminds us that God works in all situations for good for all who love the Lord (Romans 8:28).

Prayer: *Dear God in heaven, thank you for working all things to good in our lives. In Jesus' name, we pray. Amen*

Thought for the day: We can rejoice that God does not withhold good from us.

Brooke Espinoza (California, US)

Reconciliation

Read Ephesians 4:30—5:1
Be kind to one another, tender-hearted, forgiving one another, as God in Christ has forgiven you.
Ephesians 4:32 (NRSV)

My college friend Ginger and I were inseparable. We ate meals together, visited each other's families, told each other our deepest secrets and went to the same church.

After studying abroad, I decided to visit other churches. Ginger became distant and unfriendly. She stated that we could no longer be friends if I went to a different church. I was hurt, frustrated and anxious to change her mind. How could she believe that we could not be friends because we went to different churches?

Months later, I realised that her church was encouraging members to become exclusive. I was thankful that God led me to leave that church, though I mourned the loss of my friend. I continued praying for Ginger. I emailed her Bible verses. I ached for our companionship.

Six years later, I received a message from Ginger. She was sorry for cutting off our friendship. She was no longer part of the church I had left and realised that God's love isn't limited to one church or congregation. I forgave her, and I rejoice that we are friends again. God's expansive love can inspire us to forgiveness and reconciliation.

Prayer: *Dear God, help us forgive one another. Reconcile relationships that have been torn apart, and teach us to love as you love. In Jesus' holy name, we pray. Amen*

Thought for the day: As God forgave us, let us forgive one another.

Susie Baker (South Carolina, US)

The Good Shepherd

Read John 10:7–14

Christ also suffered once for sins, the righteous for the unrighteous, to bring you to God.
1 Peter 3:18 (NIV)

My wife and I were on holiday a few years ago in the country and the place where we were staying overlooked a sheep pasture. The sheep were free to roam the fields and hills, but a fence kept them within the bounds of safety.

One morning we awoke and saw that someone had left the gate open. Sheep were wandering about all over the place, and some were in danger. Soon the shepherd came, closed the gate and rounded them up until they were all safely within the enclosure.

Reflecting on the above verses reminded me of the Good Shepherd, who came to bring us safely back to God. He went to great lengths for us in suffering on the cross and dying as our substitute. Only because of what Christ endured can we know with confidence that we can enjoy the safety of the shepherd's care and attention.

Following the Good Shepherd can be challenging. But the words of 1 Peter remind us that Christ had experienced much human suffering even though he was not guilty. Christ knows what we are going through. This letter encourages us to keep living faithful lives for Christ.

Prayer: *Thank you, loving God, for the gift of your Son who leads us safely back to you. Amen*

Thought for the day: When we stray, the Good Shepherd leads us safely back to God.

Mark Wallace (Suffolk, England)

Meal Ministry

Read 1 Kings 17:8–16

Jesus said, 'I have set you an example, that you also should do as I have done to you.'
John 13:15 (NRSV)

For me, cooking has never been easy. I have no natural talent for creating beautiful, tasty dishes for my family. Because of my continued failures in the kitchen, cooking soon became a stressful chore to be dreaded.

I began to pray daily, asking God to provide me with patience and talent, but his answer was not more talent. It was a change of attitude. God revealed that providing nutritious food for my family is a ministry. As shown in the Bible, a ministry is not always easy and does not have to be perfect to be effective. Tying a shoe, washing a dish, writing a letter, mowing a lawn—these are all activities that minister to someone's basic need with kindness, love and compassion. If Jesus ministered to his disciples by washing their feet, I reasoned, is it really so unpleasant for me to cook a meal?

I re-entered my kitchen with a new attitude of ministry, not misery, and the results have been amazing. The time I spend preparing and cleaning all speak to the true nature of Jesus' love for us, an attitude of service that we pass on to the ones we love and that they in turn pass on to others. My meals are far from perfect, but they are served with hands and heart that show God's love in action.

Prayer: *O Lord, strengthen us as we minister to others. Amen*

Thought for the day: We show God's love when we minister to others.

Wendy Baker (North Carolina, US)

PRAYER FOCUS: THOSE WHO PREPARE OUR MEALS   91

Pressured to Lean

Read 2 Thessalonians 1:1–8

[God will] give relief to you who are troubled, and to us as well.
2 Thessalonians 1:7 (NIV)

A hiking stick is a hiker's best friend. On hikes in the mountains over steep paths covered with rocks and roots, my hiking stick relieves knee pressure while I am going uphill, slows me down while descending, and keeps me from falling when my feet slip. Once, when I dropped my hiking stick and it started to fall out of my reach, I didn't hesitate to hurry after it to retrieve it.

Some believe God is a crutch to lean on when we can't handle life's pressures, but I readily admit I can't handle life's pressures alone. I can do all things with Christ (see Philippians 4:13), but I make a mess on my own.

I have learned to lean on God for rest, guidance, strength and wisdom to take the next step and to know how to respond. It also reminds me that this world is not my home. One day I'll live in an eternal heaven where God will relieve the pressures I face now, but until then I must lean. When pressures come, we can stretch upward and lean forward toward God.

Prayer: *Merciful God, thank you that no burden we bear is more than your shoulders can handle if we turn to you in faith. Amen*

Thought for the day: Burdens are always lighter when we share them with God.

Martin Wiles (South Carolina, US)

Expunged Record

Read Romans 3:21–26

Have mercy on me, O God, according to your steadfast love; according to your abundant mercy blot out my transgressions.
Psalm 51:1 (NRSV)

Our state recently passed a law that will expunge certain criminal records. Applicants who are approved may leave court with a clean slate.

As a probation officer, I once went through my files to see which offenders qualified to have some of their rights restored. I was given a checklist of requirements on which to base my judgment. Once I came to a disqualifying factor, I put the file back in the drawer. The process was cut and dried.

I am glad that God doesn't have a list of disqualifying factors before expunging our records. He doesn't say, 'Sorry, your sin is too awful', or 'Look, you did this more than once. Your whole life is marked with a pattern of wrongdoing.'

There is no record that God cannot expunge. There is no life so messed up that he cannot restore it. And once our record is expunged, we can maintain a clean record with confession and forgiveness.

Prayer: *Dear Lord, we are eternally grateful for your forgiveness. We were without hope. Thank you, Jesus. Amen*

Thought for the day: God can erase any sin.

Thomas Buice (Tennessee, US)

In Difficult Times

Read Psalm 43:3–5

'I know the plans I have for you,' declares the Lord, 'plans to prosper you and not to harm you, plans to give you hope and a future.'
Jeremiah 29:11 (NIV)

I received a phone call that turned my world upside down. The fear of cancer encompassed my daily life. Through doctor's appointments, tests and awaited results, I seemed to be living in a dark tunnel. I could not see, could not plan and could not focus on simple daily tasks. As darkness threatened to pull me under, I found that I was completely dependent on God.

The more I leaned on God, the more peace I felt. He was my light in the darkness. I realised that the question I should ask was not 'Why me?', but 'Why not me?' Can't God use every circumstance in our lives for a greater purpose? My prayers were transformed. I no longer asked God to take the cancer from me. I asked him to use my cancer diagnosis for his greater good.

God answered my prayer, giving me peace as well as the desire and ability to walk with others through their experiences with cancer. He gave me gifts of encouragement, compassion, love and care so that I could reach out with understanding and support for others.

Prayer: *Thank you, dear God, for guiding us in our daily lives and for carrying us through difficult times. Amen*

Thought for the day: Our struggles give us the opportunity to show God's love to others.

Deborah Pow (Alberta, Canada)

Calloused Feet, Calloused Hearts

Read Ezekiel 36:24–28

The Lord God says, 'I will give you a new heart and put a new spirit in you; I will remove from you your heart of stone and give you a heart of flesh.'
Ezekiel 36:26 (NIV)

Growing up in Hawaii, I didn't have to wear shoes to school until the fifth year. This meant that for all those years, I never wore shoes at all. And I didn't need them, because the soles of my feet were as tough as any shoe leather. Whether I was walking on the rough asphalt of the street or the coarse sand of the beach, my feet were so calloused that I never felt any discomfort. But I also missed out on the joy of the springy softness of a lush lawn under my toes. Hardened soles lose all feeling, for good or ill.

The same can be true of our hearts. As feet can be toughened by years of contact with rough surfaces, our hearts can be hardened through years of contact with the rocky road of life's experiences. We can become so tough and cynical that we have trouble experiencing the joy of God's love and acceptance. Our souls can become so hardened by turning away from pain—our own and that of others—that there is no longer any room in our hearts for the joy we can find in Christ.

When we see areas of our lives where we have become insensitive, we can pray and read God's word to allow him to show us ways to reach out to others and share Christ's love.

Prayer: *Dear Father, soften our hearts so we can accept you and your joy in our lives. Amen*

Thought for the day: God can soften even the toughest heart.

David Ladd (Virginia, US)

Connecting, Not Communicating

Read Psalm 145:17–19

Look to the Lord and his strength; seek his face always.

1 Chronicles 16:11 (NIV)

'It's good to hear your voice, Kathleen,' my friend said. 'I'm so glad you took the time to call me.' That simple statement made me realise that too often I use fingertip technology, and not meaningful conversation, to stay in touch with family and friends. Facebook, emails and texting allow me to post photos or send short blasts of information to people I care about but don't see very often. We may be staying connected, but I'm not sure we're really communicating.

This experience made me wonder how well I'm staying in touch with God. Busy with chores and responsibilities, I try to remember to thank or praise God when particular blessings come during the day. But often I feel that even though I'm connected to God I'm not really communicating because I'm not setting aside the quiet prayer time that keeps me mindful of his word in my life.

Prayer is our direct line to God who longs to hear our 'voices'. Technology has its place in connecting us to others, but we need real conversation to strengthen and maintain any relationship—especially with God.

Prayer: *Dear God, slow us down so that finding prayer time with you becomes a priority. Keep us focused so that our conversation builds a stronger relationship with you. Amen*

Thought for the day: How much time do I spend talking and listening to God?

Kathleen Armentano (North Carolina, US)

No One Understands?

Read Hebrews 4:14–16

The Word became flesh and made his dwelling among us. We have seen his glory, the glory of the one and only Son, who came from the Father, full of grace and truth.

John 1:14 (NIV)

At times we may feel all alone and that no one understands what we are going through. That's when we have forgotten that Jesus became fully human and experienced life as we do. He was tempted as we are. He dealt with grief and sadness. He also felt joy and happiness. He shared intimate moments with close friends. The only thing Jesus didn't experience was sin; but because he paid the price of sin, he knew the suffering of sin's consequences.

Whenever we feel that no one understands, we can remember that Jesus does. God sends people into our lives to be with us and to help us. What we experience today may help us to help another person tomorrow. As we receive grace, we can extend grace. We do not need to bear our burdens alone. We can allow Christ to work in our lives and use us to work in someone else's life. We are not alone. Not only do we have Christ, we also have each other.

Prayer: *Dear God, we pray for your strength. Please let us feel your presence when we are alone. Help us to accept the compassion of those you send to us in Christ's name. As Jesus taught us, we pray, 'Father, hallowed be your name, your kingdom come. Give us each day our daily bread. Forgive us our sins, for we also forgive everyone who sins against us. And lead us not into temptation.'* Amen*

Thought for the day: Jesus understands and is with me always.

Jason Ponzio (Georgia, US)

* Luke 11:2–4 (NIV)

Look Above

Read Revelation 7:13–17

They worship [God] day and night in his temple, and the one seated on the throne will shelter them.
Revelation 7:15 (CEB)

It was sunset on a Friday when my husband and I completed our long-awaited patio, and we were exhausted. As we sat together on the patio celebrating our achievement, we faced the back of our house. 'I don't think I've ever noticed this view of our house, have you?' I asked. 'Look above the house,' he said, pointing at the huge oak tree hanging over the roof.

We built our house so that this 100-year-old oak would be in our front garden because the trunk was so beautiful, but now we were seeing it from a different view. All those years, I thought, all those problems and blessings we shared together in this house, and I never noticed that tree sheltering us from above. It gave me a whole new perspective.

That tree reminds me of our loving Creator. Day after day, we go about our routines of working and taking care of our families, dealing with the disappointments and struggles that life presents, learning to accept the tragedies as well as the blessings of life. We tend to forget that through it all God is with us, cares for us and loves us unconditionally. And when we do acknowledge him with praise for the glory of it all, we gain a totally new perspective.

Prayer: *Dear God, help us to glorify you in all that we do today so that others will see your glory through us. Amen*

Thought for the day: Today I will look above my circumstances to the one who loves and cares for all of us.

Annette McGhee (Alabama, US)

Who Will Roll the Stone Away?

Read Mark 16:1–7

[The women] asked each other, 'Who will roll the stone away from the entrance of the tomb?'
Mark 16:3 (NIV)

As a little girl, I adored my father. When he and my mother were in their eighties, my family and I enjoyed having them living with us. One evening, my dad had a massive stroke. In hospital, he made minimal progress; so he was admitted to a nursing home. I feared the prospect of facing life without him.

During Dad's remaining four months, my mother was amazing. At times, she became weary and worried about the future; but she quickly regained her strength and faith. I marvelled at her ability to do so, and she explained. Whenever she became fearful, she thought of the women who made their way to Jesus' tomb. Worried about how they would move the massive stone and enter the tomb, they asked each other, 'Who will roll the stone away?' When they arrived at the tomb, the stone had been rolled away from the entrance. God had not only provided the solution to their worry, but had given a gift that was beyond all hope.

Throughout my father's illness, when my mother or I began to worry, we reminded each other, 'Who will roll the stone away?' Then, we smiled, knowing we could trust God to help us along the way.

Prayer: *Dear Father, when we fear the future, help us to trust you completely. Amen*

Thought for the day: God will roll the stone away.

Judi F. Light (Pennsylvania, US)

Service with Love

Read Matthew 25:31–46

The king will say, 'I was hungry and you gave me food, I was thirsty and you gave me something to drink, I was a stranger and you welcomed me.'

Matthew 25:35 (NRSV)

Lately, our church has been preparing hot meals for people who are hungry or homeless. But this is not the first time we have had a ministry to poor people. In the past, when we did not have our own building, the young people collected bags of food and distributed them. We went around the neighbouring areas and sought out those who needed food. Now we have our own building where we can invite people in and feed them with hot soup, sandwiches and tea. On the first night, only one man came.

Part of me was disappointed; we had prepared a meal for 20 people. However, I noticed a difference between the church and a business project: numbers are not as important as the quality of the achieved result. But what is the point in having large numbers of guests if I didn't even know how to talk to our one guest or conduct myself around him?

I know that Jesus would have done things differently. He calls us to feed those who are hungry and welcome strangers as if we are welcoming him. Jesus would have found the right words that night. I know that with a tiny bit of faith and courage we can follow Jesus' example.

Prayer: *Dear God of Compassion, help us offer hospitality to our neighbour without fear or hesitation. Amen*

Thought for the day: When we welcome others we are welcoming God.

Anton Kuzmin (St Petersburg, Russia)

Calling Pigs

Read John 10:1–5

When [the shepherd] has brought out all his own, he goes ahead of them, and the sheep follow him because they know his voice.
John 10:4 (NRSV)

As a little girl on the farm I was responsible for feeding the pigs; so I learned how to call them to the fence for their feast. Years later, when my family visited a working farm open to the public, my knowledge of calling pigs came in handy. As we strolled along a wide path, we saw people standing on the fence, shouting and waving their arms. A herd of pigs huddled under the shade of a distant tree. The people were trying frantically to get the pigs to come to the fence. I calmly climbed up on the fence and used my knowledge. The whole herd of pigs came running to the fence. The tourists asked, 'How did you do that?' I explained simply, 'They knew the distinctive call and responded.'

The same is true for followers of Christ. When we hear the distinctive call of the one who knows us by name, we respond because we know his voice. John 10:5 says, 'They will not follow a stranger… because they do not know the voice of strangers.' We hear many voices in our lives, but only one, the voice of Jesus Christ our Lord, can lead us to the eternal feast.

Prayer: *Good Shepherd, when we hear you calling us by name, let us run to you for everything we need. Amen*

Thought for the day: The Lord is my shepherd, and he knows me by name.

Xavia Sheffield (Maryland, US)

Road to Health

Read Hebrews 5:11–14
Everyone who lives on milk, being still an infant, is unskilled in the word of righteousness.
Hebrews 5:13 (NRSV)

A mother brought her rather thin child to our clinic. She had weaned him at one year of age. I asked her what she was feeding him now. She said, 'Tea without milk and cornmeal porridge.' I asked to see the child's 'Road to Health Chart', a medical chart that includes a very useful graph indicating how the child is gaining weight over time in comparison with all children of that age. This child had stopped gaining weight and was heading for malnutrition, a most serious condition. I explained to his mother what to feed him, emphasising foods high in protein to supplement the carbohydrates in his diet.

In Hebrews we read of Christians who were suffering from spiritual malnutrition and therefore had stopped growing. This too is a serious condition. Christian spiritual growth is aimed at ultimately attaining the likeness of our Saviour. Our nourishment comes from studying God's word and daily prayer contact with Jesus, who described himself as the bread of life. Jesus promised that those who come to him and believe in him would never go spiritually hungry or thirsty (see John 6:35).

Prayer: *Loving God, give us a new hunger for your word. Help us to be faithful in prayer and petition with thanksgiving. In Jesus' name we pray. Amen*

Thought for the day: Are we gaining weight on the 'spiritual health' chart?

John McCutcheon (Limpopo, South Africa)

Every Day Grace

Read Matthew 13:1–9, 18–23
In [Jesus Christ] we have redemption through his blood, the forgiveness of sins, in accordance with the riches of God's grace that he lavished on us.
Ephesians 1:7–8 (NIV)

I spent a relaxing day planting petunias of different shades of pink and red interspersed with salvia. I imagined how much I was going to enjoy caring for and watching them thrive. A week later, after returning from holiday, I approached my flower-bed with some trepidation. I stopped, amazed. How could the flower-bed get so full of weeds in such a short time?

I started pulling up weeds with a vengeance. Some of them were quite large while others were just starting. Some had grown so close to the plants that I had to wrestle them free to avoid damaging the blooms.

These weeds reminded me of my sin. When I neglect to confess and release it to God, my sin overpowers my ability to blossom and grow. Every day I need to take care of sin before it takes root. If I wait for Sunday worship to confess and release my sin, I may have given it time to overtake me. Left alone, sin can grow like weeds that need to be pulled every day. And every day, God's grace is enough.

Prayer: *Loving God, help us to pay attention to sin in our lives. Thank you for the grace you lavish on us when we confess and repent. Amen*

Thought for the day: God's grace is always enough.

Cindy Curtis (South Carolina, US)

God's Glory

Read Job 36: 26–33

In golden splendour God comes in awesome majesty.
Job 37:22 (NIV)

Mourning the death of my husband, I was distraught. The world as I knew it had changed. I wandered to the window and gazed at the park below.

Struck by the intensity of the golden light in the park, my heart leapt. The buildings, made from ochre stone, were bathed in golden light. The trees' branches were almost bare, but still stippled with bronze leaves. Distantly the sea, frequently drab grey, became an intense turquoise.

Then storm clouds gathered above, assuming an amber tint, and a rainbow arched across the sky. Rain, and then hail, rattled the windows. But I had already captured the vision and wept at its beauty before I watched it fade from sight.

In James 1:17 we read: 'Every good and perfect gift is from above, coming down from the Father of the heavenly lights, who does not change like shifting shadows'. Seasons change. Weather changes. Lives change. But the Lord our God is steadfast and true; his love never changes. In the midst of life's storms, we are surrounded by God's glory.

Prayer: *Thank you, Lord, that your love is always there whatever our circumstances. Amen*

Thought for the day: The Lord never changes.

Pauline Pullan (North Yorkshire, England)

Daily Tasks

Read Acts 2:36–42
Everything that God created is good, and nothing is to be rejected if it is received with thanksgiving, because it is consecrated by the word of God and prayer.
1 Timothy 4:4–5 (NIV)

'Where are my socks?' was the plaintive cry from my daughter. I hear this plea often in the rush of getting everyone off to work and school in the morning. Sometimes, in the midst of our busy lives, we feel that we do not have enough time to meditate and praise God. Sweeping the floor, making beds, washing clothes, cooking meals—these required daily tasks seem endless.

Being a homemaker reminds me that God also expects daily tasks from us. Having a daily devotional time and praying without ceasing (see 1 Thessalonians 5:17) helps us to maintain our faith and the well-being of our souls. Keeping our faith new and fresh requires daily renewal. By taking the time to worship by praise and prayer each morning, we are being good housekeepers of our souls. However, rather than being the chore that housework can become, this daily communion with our Maker always brings us joy.

Prayer: *Dear God, as we struggle in our busy lives, help us to find time for the joy of communion with you—our Lord and our Maker. Amen*

Thought for the day: As we daily communicate with God, we can better see the way he works in our everyday activities.

Mariella Carr (Texas, US)

Help with Burdens

Read Matthew 11:28–30

Jesus said, 'Come to me, all you who are weary and burdened, and I will give you rest.'

Matthew 11:28 (NIV)

Like many in my generation, I am taking care of elderly parents. I have sole responsibility for my mum since my brother lives some miles away. I work hard to make sure she is taken care of and that all her needs are met. The situation is more difficult because my mum and I have never had a great relationship, but I know that taking care of her is the right thing to do. I want to honour her by doing the best I can, but most of the time, I am overwhelmed. I have the rest of my family to look after. I also have some issues with my own health and self-esteem. I look at all that I need to accomplish, and I don't know where to start. Do I work at home? Do I go to my mum's house and get it ready to sell? Do I spend time with God, knowing that he guides me to do what is right for mum and for me? When I am tired and need to rest, I fall back on Matthew 11:28.

I am thankful that God is always waiting to comfort me and reassure me that I am doing well. The world may be saying, 'Why aren't you doing more?' but God lets me know that all I need to do is my best. I rest in the comfort of his love when taking care of Mum gets to be too much.

Prayer: *Thank you, Lord, for being with us and for giving comfort and rest to the weary. Amen*

Thought for the day: Rest is just a prayer away.

Susie Hoffmann (Ohio, US)

Watch the Light

Read John 1:1–14

If I say, 'Surely the darkness shall cover me, and the light around me become night,' even the darkness is not dark to you; the night is as bright as the day, for darkness is as light to you.
Psalm 139:11–12 (NRSV)

Our son-in-law, a professional photographer, was to film a football game at a stadium he had never visited. Relying on his knowledge of the area and the technology in his vehicle, he set out. He drove anxiously through darkness to numerous dead ends, finally accepting that he was lost. He stopped, got out of the car and looked around. There in the distance he saw the stadium lights' glow. Watching the light, he drove steadily toward it.

Sometimes in our life's journey we struggle to find the way. We rely on knowledge, education and our sense of control. But inevitably, we come to dead ends trying to find our way through pain, relationships and even worship or church responsibilities. As life darkens, we may feel frustrated, helpless and lost, forgetting the light that God shines on the path to lead us.

Where is that light? It is in prayer, in meditation and in reading God's word. Sometimes this light shines as clearly as from the strong lights of a stadium; sometimes we have just enough to see the next step on our path. Either way, when we rely on God we can move ahead with confidence that he is with us, lighting the way.

Prayer: *Giver of light, we admit that we are in darkness; we are lost without daily light from you. Help us to see your light and to follow. Amen*

Thought for the day: God lights our path one step at a time.

Bettie Higgins (Alabama, US)

Loving the Unlovable

Read 1 Peter 3:8–13

Jesus said, 'By this everyone will know that you are my disciples, if you love one another.'
John 13:35 (NIV)

A few years ago, I served a seven-month jail sentence for drink-driving. Within the first two weeks of my incarceration, I escaped two stabbing attempts and became the victim of extortion. That was only the beginning. Regularly, I witnessed the strong preying on the weak: food taken by force, verbal intimidation used to cut in lines, blankets stolen on bone-chilling winter nights. I hid in my ten-foot by eight-foot cell, wishing that the bullies would disappear into a bottomless pit.

Reading the Bible given to me by a sympathetic guard changed all that. Certain passages—about loving my brother and treating others the way I would like to be treated—seemed to light up my space like neon lights. For twelve hours a day, I read my Bible, prayed and asked God to reveal how I had come to stray so far. During this journey, God transformed my heart, enabling me to love all the often-unlovable people in my life. I was able to pray for my enemies.

We are to love unconditionally everywhere our foot makes an imprint. This great assignment God has entrusted to us as Christians may often feel like an anchor around our necks. But when we allow God to love others through us, we can be wonderfully transformed in the process.

Prayer: *Dear God, help us love others as you love them. Amen*

Thought for the day: When we love others unconditionally, we are blessed as much as they.

Avon White (Tennessee, US)

I Almost Missed It!

Read 2 Kings 5:1–19

Naaman went away angry and said, 'I thought that [Elisha] would surely come out to me and stand and call on the name of the Lord his God, wave his hand over the spot and cure me of my leprosy.'
2 Kings 5:11 (NIV)

My husband often has difficulty finding things, even though I've told him exactly where they are. 'Where is the milk?' he asks, while staring into the refrigerator. 'Second shelf on the right,' I reply. 'I don't see it,' he complains. Finally, I walk over and point to where it sits. 'Oh, I was looking for a cardboard carton,' he explains. Sometimes a different colour or size of a package causes him not to be able to 'see' the object in question.

My husband's 'blindness' reminds me of the story of Naaman. He expected Elisha to cure him in a certain way. When the cure came in a different form, he didn't recognise it. He almost left without being healed! Fortunately for Naaman, he had a servant who 'opened his eyes' and encouraged him to try this unexpected method—and his healing came.

How often do we miss out on God's blessings because they don't come in the form we expect? We can't imagine 'that person' or 'that experience' bringing a blessing from him. May we open our minds and hearts to God's gifts and guidance in whatever 'package' they might come.

Prayer: *Dear Lord, you have plans for us greater than we can imagine. Help us not to limit you by the smallness of our minds and the rigidity of our expectations. Amen*

Thought for the day: If we open our eyes, God's blessings are right in front of us!

Debra Callaway (Kansas, US)

Asleep on the Job?

Read Mark 4:35–41

Blessed is the one who perseveres under trial because, having stood the test, that person will receive the crown of life that the Lord has promised to those who love him.

James 1:12 (NIV)

Following our worship service, one member of our congregation offered a different perspective on today's story of Jesus' calming the storm. Usually, we affirm Jesus' divinity by focusing on verse 41: 'Who is this? Even the wind and waves obey him!' This time, we paused at verse 38, in which the disciples find Jesus sleeping, wake him, and ask, 'Don't you care if we drown?' (Mark 4:38).

All of us can relate to the disciples' frustration. 'Jesus, you calmed a storm, fed the 5,000, and raised the dead; where were you today when 15,000 children died of hunger? Where were you for all the months I prayed for work and doors closed in my face? Jesus, wake up! 'Don't you care if we drown?'

Before we doubt what we cannot understand, we can recall that Jesus died on a cross for us. Christ knows that 'the whole creation has been groaning' for redemption (Romans 8:22). Even when we are so broken that words will not come, the Holy Spirit hears our prayers and intercedes for us with God (see Romans 8:26).

Prayer: *Giver of every good and perfect gift, help us. Heal our unbelief. Amen*

Thought for the day: Jesus showed his love for us through his death and resurrection.

Dan Nelson (North Carolina, US)

The Way to Eternal Life

Read John 14:1–10

Jesus said to [Thomas], 'I am the way and the truth and the life. No one comes to the Father except through me.'
John 14:6 (NIV)

I was late for an appointment when I decided to call a taxi. On the phone the driver insisted that he knew where to pick me up and wouldn't listen to my directions. But a while later he called back, having lost his way. Now quite worried, I again gave him directions, using a well-known university as a reference point. Again, he confirmed that he knew the place and promised to be there in a short while. But he got lost a second time.

After several such conversations, the driver finally arrived. The signposts to my location were all very clear, but the driver had been unable to follow any of them correctly.

Reflecting back on this incident, I realise that we are much like this driver in our spiritual lives. Similar to Thomas and Philip in today's reading, we rely on our own knowledge when we actually do not know the way. We have the holy Bible, the living word of God to guide us through all circumstances in life, but often we follow its guidance only after we have lost our way. With God's grace, we can look for guidance and live in right relationship with Christ.

Prayer: *Heavenly Father, thank you for your continued love and care for us even when we fail to listen to you. In Jesus' name we pray. Amen*

Thought for the day: The Bible is our guide for life.

Philip Polo (Nairobi, Kenya)

PRAYER FOCUS: TAXI DRIVERS

Hundreds of Dresses

Read Matthew 25:14–30

The master said, 'Well done, good and faithful servant! You have been faithful with a few things; I will put you in charge of many things. Come and share your master's happiness!'

Matthew 25:23 (NIV)

When I was a child my mother taught me to sew, but at that age I considered that sewing was very boring. Then a couple of years ago, God made me aware of a need through an international relief organisation and of my responsibility to use my skills to bless others. So I phoned my mother, and together we started sewing. In two months' time, we had 120 dresses ready to ship to Haiti. The following year, with the help of more than 50 friends and acquaintances, we sewed and shipped 440 more.

I am amazed at the way God used my sewing skills to start something bigger than I could have imagined. When I used my God-given talents in this project, he helped me to bless children in another country. Over time, others were also drawn into this ongoing ministry. I don't know how many dresses and shorts we will ship this year, but I do know that each of us is blessed when we use our talents for God's glory.

Prayer: *Dear Lord, help us to be aware of the talents you have given to us and to look for ways to use them to serve you. Amen*

Thought for the day: God has bigger plans for our gifts than we can imagine.

Kim Harms (Iowa, US)

Healing Prayers

Read James 5:13–16
The prayer offered in faith will make the sick person well; the Lord will raise them up.
James 5:15 (NIV)

For years I worked as a cardio-thoracic surgical nurse, preparing and sending people to heart bypass surgery. Twenty-four hours after surgery patients returned to our ward with tubes and drips and often in considerable discomfort. Each shift my patients were randomly assigned to me by a nurse on the previous shift, so I never knew exactly who they were until I received my assignment. So I developed a strict habit of praying for each of my patients during my 30-minute commute to the hospital each day. Even if I didn't know who those patients would be, there was great peace in knowing that God knew.

Heart bypass surgery is often a frightening experience for my patients; they know their heart will be temporarily stopped while being repaired by human hands. Seeing their fear, I have often asked if they wanted me to pray for them. No one has ever refused. I never knew my patients' spiritual background, but I did find a common human need for God's comfort and healing power. Knowing I was praying for them seemed to give my patients a visible peace. Psalm 29:11 says, 'The Lord gives strength to his people; the Lord blesses his people with peace' (NIV).

Prayer: *Dear Father God, help us always to be sensitive to the fears and needs of others and to strengthen them with your word. Amen*

Thought for the day: Through prayer God offers us comfort and healing.

Debbi Whitezell (Pennsylvania, US)

God's Child

Read John 13:1–13

The Son of Man came not to be served but to serve, and to give his life a ransom for many.

Mark 10:45 (NRSV)

When our family moved to a new city I had trouble finding employment. Eventually, I accepted a low-paying, part-time position cleaning the local library. What I hoped would be a temporary job has lasted over a year. The longer I have worked in this job, the more I felt stuck and the more my self-esteem plummeted. I was embarrassed by the work I did and grew bitter and resentful.

While studying the Bible one morning, I read about Jesus washing the feet of his disciples—a task usually performed by the lowliest of servants. This illustration reminded me that Jesus set an example of servanthood for us to follow. I realised that my ego had been telling me that my job was beneath me, and I had been measuring my worth by the world's standards, not God's. As I pondered Jesus' example, my focus began to shift.

This job has taught me humility. Creating a clean and inviting atmosphere in the library is an important service. My pay has helped to alleviate financial strain for my family and the flexible, part-time hours allow me more time at home with my young son. Even if I don't enjoy what I do, I can be proud of a job well done in service to others. I have value not because of what I do but because of who I am. I am a child of God.

Prayer: *Gracious God, help us to follow the example set by Jesus Christ to serve others joyfully. Amen*

Thought for the day: We each have unlimited value as children of God.

Julie Calleja (Michigan, US)

From Sadness to Joy

Read 2 Corinthians 1:3–7

May our Lord Jesus Christ himself and God our Father, who loved us and by his grace gave us eternal encouragement and hope, encourage your hearts and strengthen you in every good deed and word.
2 Thessalonians 2:16–17 (NIV)

Today I decided to go shopping because I felt discouraged and needed a distraction. As I walked through the crowds, I saw a couple from my church and stopped to talk with them.

Soon they were telling me about the concerns they had for a family member who didn't have a relationship with God. As I listened, I realised that when we belong to God's family we feel free to share one another's troubles. The issues they spoke of weighed heavy on their hearts, and I became so sympathetic to their story that I forgot about my own sadness. Soon I found myself encouraging them and, in doing so, my own burdens were lightened.

By the time we parted, we were all smiling. We shook hands and went our separate ways. Giving us good thoughts, encouraging words and love to share, God lifted our burdens.

Prayer: *Dear God, thank you for our brothers and sisters in Christ who share our burdens and show us your love. We pray as Jesus taught us, saying, 'Our Father which art in heaven, Hallowed be thy name. Thy kingdom come. Thy will be done in earth, as it is in heaven. Give us this day our daily bread. And forgive us our debts, as we forgive our debtors. And lead us not into temptation, but deliver us from evil: For thine is the kingdom, and the power, and the glory, forever. Amen.'**

Thought for the day: We can encourage others by inviting God to speak and act through us.

Mary Haskett (Ontario, Canada)

PRAYER FOCUS: SOMEONE WHOSE SADNESS IS OVERWHELMING
* Matthew 6:9–13 (KJV)

A Giving Heart

Read 1 Timothy 6:17–19

[Jesus] said, 'This poor widow has put in more than all the others. All these people gave their gifts out of their wealth; but she out of her poverty put in all she had to live on.'
Luke 21:3–4 (NIV)

My minister's nine-year-old son is passionate about football and loves to play the game. Once he found out that I was a player, he would ask me to play with him every time we saw each other. So, we made a deal to play football every Wednesday night in the church's grounds. One Wednesday night, as we walked down the alley to the church, I noticed that he was paying close attention to the ground as we walked. When I asked him what he was doing the boy said, 'Looking for change on the ground so I can put it in the offering.'

The Bible is full of stories and parables about money. A story that has influenced me is Luke's account about the widow's offering. When this small boy searched for dropped and forgotten change in the back alley behind our church, I couldn't help but remember this poor widow. I feel the stress of money every day, but this widow and small boy show me how to give all I have freely and generously. When we give of our money, we can be confident that God will take care of us the way he takes care of the lilies and the sparrows.

Prayer: *Thank you, dear God, for blessing us so we may bless others. Amen*

Thought for the day: Freely you have received; freely give (Matthew 10:8).

Joshua Stueve (Texas, US)

A Fountain of Grace

Read Luke 6:37–42

Give, and it will be given to you. A good measure, pressed down, shaken together and running over, will be poured into your lap. For with the measure you use, it will be measured to you.
Luke 6:38 (NIV)

In the town next to mine a giant fountain sits on the corner of a busy street. It is surrounded by steps where passersby can stop to take a break from the sun and enjoy the cool mist that floats up out of the water and dances in the air. The water gushes forward, splashes down into a pool, then trickles down to a shallower one from where it drains and eventually recycles. People flock to it every day, enjoying the simple beauty of the fresh well-spring.

I drove past the fountain one day just as I happened to offer a prayer of thanks for everything in my life. God gives to me generously, showering me with love, mercy and especially grace. I am utterly dependent on his grace, yet I often find it hard to be graceful to others.

Seeing the cascading water reminded me that I should be willing to forgive continually, just as the water in that fountain flows continually to offer its refreshment. God splashes down blessings on me, soaking me with love that I do not deserve. His grace that constantly washes over me inspires me to allow it to flow through me to others.

Prayer: *Dear Father, forgive our unforgiving and condemning attitudes. Open our hearts so that they overflow with your boundless love and generosity. In Jesus' name we pray. Amen*

Thought for the day: God gives us grace—more than enough to share.

Alicia Yost (Connecticut, US)

Comfort in Our Darkest Hour

Read Mark 14:32–42

Scorn has broken my heart and has left me helpless; I looked for sympathy, but there was none, for comforters, but I found none.
Psalm 69:20 (NIV)

How alone Jesus must have felt on the night before his death! His disciples couldn't even stay awake to keep him company in prayer. That night, one of his closest friends betrayed him.

I've had my share of times when I felt lost and when I felt a heavy burden deep within me. Finding people who would listen to my cries wasn't easy. Most people are already overwhelmed with their own burdens and they don't have energy to share someone else's.

We have all experienced times of brokenness: broken hearts, lost jobs, failing health, the death of loved ones. In these times, we need all the support we can get. We need friends who will listen without getting tired and family members who will stay with us when we can't sleep.

Like us, Jesus must have looked for comfort. He must have wanted support from those he loved, but he found no sympathy. Only in the Father did he find strength to carry on. He cried out his deepest fears, knowing that God would not judge him but love and support him all the way. We can do the same.

Prayer: *God of all comfort, when we can find no sympathy from the people around us, may we turn our eyes to you, our hope. Amen*

Thought for the day: Even when we feel abandoned, God is always our friend.

Jocelyn Soriano (Manila, Philippines)

Present Tense

Read John 5:19–24

Jesus said, 'Anyone who hears my word and believes him who sent me has eternal life, and does not come under judgment, but has passed from death to life.'
John 5:24 (NRSV)

Recently, my wife and I took a course in personal finance to try to be prepared for our retirements in about ten years. The basic lesson was that we have to sacrifice now to have a better future. Then, when I went to the doctor, he urged me to go on a diet and lose weight. The message was the same: I need to sacrifice pleasure now for a better future.

Some people consider the Christian life as a third example of sacrificing now for a better future. But I believe scripture presents a different view. In this passage from John, Jesus tells us that eternal life and passing from death to life is a present-tense reality. When we believe in and follow Christ, we already have eternal life; we do not have to wait for it at some later date.

The abundant life that Jesus offers (see John 10:10) is not something we have to wait until physical death to receive. It is here now, in the present tense.

Prayer: *Our Lord Jesus Christ, thank you for the abundant, eternal life that we have in you now. Amen*

Thought for the day: We gain eternal life as soon as we believe in and follow Christ.

Michael Macdonald (North Carolina, US)

Seeing with New Eyes

Read Isaiah 61:1–3

Jesus read from the Book of Isaiah, '[The Spirit of the Lord] has sent me to proclaim… recovery of sight to the blind.'
Luke 4:18 (NRSV)

One spring I decided to visit my sister on South Africa's West Coast to see the famous display of wild flowers. At mid-morning my sister and I drove directly into the morning sun. I glanced around eagerly but my spirits dropped; the country was clothed in a drab grey-green. 'The best flowers are up ahead,' said my sister with a twinkle in her eye. I stared forward. Nothing! Then my sister pulled over and made a 180-degree turn. I gasped with disbelief! As far as the eye could see the countryside was clothed in a dazzling tapestry of orange, white and yellow daisies.

'They were there all the time,' explained my sister. 'These daisies are true "sun-flowers". They close up at night or in overcast weather, but when the sun shines they all turn their faces toward the sun. Driving here, we could see only the drab undersides.' It was as if I had been blind, but now I could see!

As I pondered this, I remembered that Jesus came to bring recovery of sight to the blind. So often our focus is on the gloomy negatives of life. We need to come to Jesus and let him make a 180-degree turn in our attitudes. That is when he gives us 'beauty for ashes, the oil of joy for mourning, the garment of praise for the spirit of heaviness' (Isaiah 61:3, KJV).

Prayer: *Dear Lord, open our eyes that we may see the beauty of your creation and the wonderful love you have for us. Amen*

Thought for the day: God's glory is evident in the beauty of creation.

Gerald McCann (Cape Town, South Africa)

Divine Guidance

Read Job 9:8–10

[God] is the maker of the Bear and Orion, the Pleiades and the constellations of the south.
Job 9:9 (NIV)

One of my favourite activities after a hectic day is to go outside after dinner, when all is quiet, and gaze at the evening sky. On a clear night many stars and constellations are visible, such as the Pleiades and the Plough. But my favourite has always been Orion—maybe because its outline and belt are so distinct in the sky.

Recently, my Bible study group was studying the book of Job. When I read Job 9:9, it occurred to me that the constellations have been around since Creation. The ancients looked upon them with the same awe and reverence that I look upon them today. In the same way, God has been there since the beginning, and he is with us today. He is unchanging; the God who spoke to Job is the same God to whom I pray every night.

In our busy lives, it is easy to get caught up by stress and anxiety and let the One who has the power to relieve them go unnoticed—or forgotten. The mariners of old used the stars to guide them because they were a constant. Our constant is he who created those same stars—the unchanging God who will be with us all the days of our life's journey.

Prayer: *Dear Lord, thank you for being our light and our guide through every circumstance of life. Amen*

Thought for the day: No matter how lost we may be, God can find us.

Wallace Brixner, Jr (New Jersey, US)

From Generation to Generation

Read Isaiah 43:18–21

I will sing of the Lord's great love forever; with my mouth I will make your faithfulness known through all generations.
Psalm 89:1 (NIV)

Generation after generation, we carry forward both favourable and unfavourable family traits. As we mature, we tell younger generations about the mistakes we have made in our lives and try to demonstrate the behaviour we hope they will follow.

Recently, the fourth generation arrived in our family in the form of a healthy baby girl. Representing the oldest living generation, I reflected upon the current mental and spiritual health of our family. While many of our family members have suffered from worry and depression, they have exhibited their faith and strength in successfully overcoming these afflictions as they sought God's help through professional counselling. Faith in God has been a family trait for generations and is now being introduced to the next.

Watching a family member repeat the mistakes of the past is difficult. But we live in the faith and the hope that those before us taught—those who distributed the yeast which is slowly working to produce healthier spiritual lives. By being faithful to God and trying to live in the right way, we are slowly recognising God's 'new thing' (Isaiah 43:19) in our family.

Prayer: *Dear Lord, we thank you that you are trustworthy throughout all generations. Amen*

Thought for the day: What am I teaching about God to the next generation?

Cynthia Piazza (New York, US)

Looking on the Outside

Read 1 Samuel 16:1–13

The Lord searcheth all hearts, and understandeth all the imaginations of the thoughts.
1 Chronicles 28:9 (KJV)

When I went to the shop, I requested a clean-looking gas cylinder for our home stove. The manager obliged, and I was happy to receive a bright red cylinder that looked almost new. When I connected it to the gas stove at home, a hissing sound warned me that gas might be leaking. The smell of gas confirmed my fear. I went back to the store to exchange the cylinder for another one. This time I did not worry about the look of the cylinder. I got an old rusty cylinder, but it did not leak and I was satisfied.

Often we place a high value on outward appearance, which does not necessarily reflect the inner state of an item or a person. Saul was a handsome person; but after he was made king of Israel, his heart turned away from God's commandments. Later, the spirit of God departed from him. God told Samuel to anoint one of the sons of Jesse as the next king of Israel. When he saw Eliab, Samuel thought he was the one God had chosen; but the Lord said that God looks not on outward appearance but on the heart. As a result, seven of Jesse's sons passed before Samuel and none was chosen. Finally, David was anointed king of Israel. It wasn't David's appearance that caused God to choose him; he was a man after God's own heart (Acts 13:22).

Prayer: *Dear God, let us see as you see, looking not on outward appearance but on the heart. Amen*

Thought for the day: God values the faithfulness of our hearts.

Pramila Barkataki (Uttar Pradesh, India)

Those Annoying Dogs

Read Luke 11:5–10
Ask and it will be given to you; seek and you will find; knock and the door will be opened to you.
Luke 11:9 (NIV)

The neighbours' dogs are at it again. Everyone knows when the neighbours are not at home because the dogs bark constantly—all day long, day after day. My attempts to scold them from over the fence only encourage them. Apparently, they perceive my actions as a standing ovation to their 'performance'—and, like a performer, they oblige with increased volume and fervour.

Even though their barking annoys me, I have grudgingly to admit that in one way they are setting a good example for me in my relationship with Christ. In today's reading Jesus encourages us to be persistent in seeking a deeper relationship with him. He calls us to ask, seek and knock. In other words, he is calling us to engage in prayer with him throughout the day—and then do it again the next day and the next. Jesus assures us that those who ask, seek and knock will strengthen their relationship with him.

One good thing about those constantly-barking dogs—they remind me to be persistent in growing in my love and devotion to Jesus.

Prayer: *Dear Lord, help us to be persistent in seeking a deep and meaningful relationship with you. Amen*

Thought for the day: It's a new day, and I want more of Jesus in it.

John Bagdanov (California, US)

Growing

Read Matthew 6:25–34

Happy are those who trust in the Lord… They will be like trees planted by the streams, whose roots reach down to the water.
Jeremiah 17:7–8 (CEB)

Twenty-five years ago, I was transferred to a mental health facility some distance from my family and friends. I had suffered from alcohol dependence and was diagnosed with schizophrenia. I greatly needed the assistance of mental health professionals.

Each year, my mother takes me to visit my relatives. On those occasions, I have grown to admire a lovely painting in the home of my aunt. It depicts a wide variety of colourful flowers. The painting has drawn me to another understanding of my life by encouraging me to grow and develop wherever God has placed me, as these magnificent blossoms have grown where they were planted. Jesus reminds us that the wild lilies of the field are not anxious about their role in life; they radiate with God's purpose by being themselves.

I find satisfaction and great joy in the place where God has planted me. I have not drunk alcohol for more than 13 years. I have developed loving relationships in the church I attend. After several changes in treatment, my medication therapy has brought about successful results. I want to be like one of the flowers in my aunt's painting, planted in this lovely family of mental health residents.

Prayer: *Dear God, help us to find peace where we are, even in the midst of trauma. Give us the power and grace to overcome mental illness and all obstacles to abundant life. Amen*

Thought for the day: We can thrive where God has planted us.

Howard David Glawson (North Carolina, US)

PRAYER FOCUS: MENTAL HEALTH PATIENTS

Taking Courage

Read Mark 6:45–52

[The disciples] all saw [Jesus] and were terrified. Immediately he spoke to them and said, 'Take courage! It is I. Don't be afraid.'
Mark 6:50 (NIV)

Our reading for today describes the disciples sailing to meet Jesus at Bethsaida and straining at the oars because the wind was against them. Panic-stricken, the disciples had tried to manage the situation, but things got out of hand. The Lord eventually came to their rescue by walking on water, right toward them. Unfortunately, the disciples did not recognise Jesus and thought they had seen a ghost. They realised it was the Lord only when he finally said to them, 'Take courage. It is I. Don't be afraid!'

Jesus was telling them to be still and to be sure. Stillness, in its truest sense, is our ability to trust that God is present and hears us in all situations. Being still is the hardest thing to do when we are in the thick of crisis or when things get out of control. But when all is said and done, learning to let go of our worries and trust that God is present shows great wisdom.

The key to being sure is perspective. Certainly, we will have our share of strong winds and rough waters in life. When these moments come, may we learn to take courage and never miss out on the presence of Jesus, the ever-faithful One who comes to us each and every time.

Prayer: *Give us true courage, O Lord, so that when the strong winds come, we may remain still and sure in your presence. Amen*

Thought for the day: True courage is learning to trust God.

Bernadette Amistoso-Morales (Negros Oriental, Philippines)

Look Up

Read Psalm 19:1–9

I lift up my eyes to the mountains—where does my help come from? My help comes from the Lord, the Maker of heaven and earth.
Psalm 121:1–2 (NIV)

One evening while on holiday, we went to an outdoor entertainment event, which culminated with our standing in darkness under a magnificent canopy of trees. We were told to close our eyes just for a moment and then to look up. When we opened our eyes, we found that hundreds of lights had been strung among the branches—an enchanting sight!

As we drove back to our accommodation through an area with no lights, we looked up to see that the whole sky was covered with brilliant stars—a sight which far exceeded the artificial light display we had seen earlier.

At all times, but especially when we are in need of comfort and assurance, it is important to lift our eyes and look beyond the cares and concerns of our earthly life that can cloud our vision. As we do, we realise that we are in the hands of the great God of the universe. He is not a distant figure, as Jesus revealed, but is here with us, sharing our lives and walking with us each day.

Prayer: *Gracious God, in every situation of our lives help us to be aware of your nearness and your love reaching out to us. Amen*

Thought for the day: God's love shines through our cares and concerns.

William David Willis (New South Wales, Australia)

What is Important in Life?

Read 2 Corinthians 12:7–10

The human spirit will endure sickness; but a broken spirit—who can bear?
Proverbs 18:14 (NRSV)

One wonderful summer morning I went out for a walk. I went in a wheelchair because this is the only way I can move. A man came up behind me and said: 'I don't envy you.' I kept going, smiling and thinking that he should envy me! What a shame, I thought, that people often don't see what is really important in life. Health problems are seen as a huge calamity while problems with the soul go unnoticed and the other gifts of God are not valued.

God has blessed me so abundantly! I live with my dad who is called the best father in the world by everyone who knows him. We have a flat, and we even each have our own room. I have friends who enrich my life. I live in a country where, after 70 years of persecuting the faith, there is now freedom of belief, and I have come to God. My daughter is studying at university and recently she and her fiancé got married in our church. I simply cannot find words of gratitude to God for all that he has given me. No, I can't walk, but I have so many other joys in my life. Most importantly, I have the Lord.

Prayer: *Dear Lord, help us to see your grace and mercy in our lives. We pray as Jesus taught us, saying, 'Our Father which art in heaven, Hallowed be thy name. Thy kingdom come. Thy will be done, as in heaven, so in earth. Give us day by day our daily bread. And forgive us our sins; for we also forgive every one that is indebted to us. And lead us not into temptation; but deliver us from evil.'* Amen*

Thought for the day: Today I will find joy in God's gifts.

Galina Samson (Voronezh, Russia)

Praying for a Friend

Read Philippians 1:3–11

We have not ceased praying for you and asking that you may be filled with the knowledge of God's will in all spiritual wisdom and understanding.

Colossians 1:9 (NRSV)

Unfounded accusations at work, a rebellious teenager, an unpaid mortgage, nagging illness—the hardships my colleague was experiencing seemed overwhelming. I listened without comment. What could I say? He surely didn't need a lecture on how to endure hardship. My heart ached for him. My mind searched for a helpful response. When he paused to take a drink of water, I said, 'I'd love to solve even one of these problems for you, but I can't. But I can and I do pray for you.' I picked up my Bible, opened it to Philippians 1, and said, 'Here's what Paul prayed for the Philippians. It's what I'm praying for you: that God will give you depth of insight so that you may be able to discern what is best, and that your behaviour in each matter will bring glory to God.'

Just hearing those words comforted my friend. He smiled and said, 'You're a good friend. I'm praying for you, too.'

'I'm always willing to listen. It helps me pray more often and more specifically for you,' I told him.

People don't usually need advice. Instead God calls us to be listeners and intercessors.

Prayer: *Dear Jesus, our great high priest, bring someone across my path today who needs to be encouraged. Amen*

Thought for the day: Who needs my attention and prayers today?

Denise Loock (North Carolina, US)

Always the Same

Read Hebrews 6:12–20
The Father of the heavenly lights... does not change like shifting shadows.
James 1:17 (NIV)

My wife, Holly, decided to surprise our daughter Jessie at her nursery school for lunch. After they had finished eating, Holly suggested a game of Telephone (also called Gossip). The first person whispers a phrase or sentence into the next person's ear. The second person passes on what they thought they heard, until all participants have received the message. Then, the last person says aloud what was said to them. Usually, the final statement is vastly different from the initial one.

Jessie started one of the rounds by whispering, 'God is always the same.' The game went on around the table, through several children, until the final statement was revealed: 'God is always the same.' The original statement had not changed at all.

James 1:17 tells us that God is steadfast, unchanging. Numbers 23:19 also speaks of God's faithfulness: 'God is not human, that he should lie... [or] change his mind. Does he speak and then not act? Does he promise and not fulfil?' (NIV). We can trust and rely on God. Over a period of several thousand years, God promised the Messiah—and that promise was fulfilled in Jesus' life, death, and resurrection. How sweet was this steadfast promise!

Prayer: *Dear God, in a constantly-changing world, remind us that you are trustworthy and that your promises never change. In Jesus' name. Amen*

Thought for the day: God is always dependable and trustworthy.

Larry Crockett (Tennessee, US)

Source of Life

Read John 15:1–8

Jesus said, 'If you do not remain in me, you are like a branch that is thrown away and withers; such branches are picked up, thrown into the fire and burned.'

John 15:6 (NIV)

West Virginia was recently hit by a big storm with high, damaging winds. Our area was one of the most severely affected, with several trees blown down and damaged.

A week later, I noticed that in such a short time the leaves of the trees left unattended had turned brown and were dying. Once they were cut off from their source of life, they were unable to live and continue to grow.

I was reminded that this is true of my spiritual life and my relationship with God. I am like the brown, wilted leaves on the trees when I fail to stay faithful with my Bible study, prayer life, active worship, and interaction with other Christians. I have become removed from the source of life—Jesus Christ and my relationship with God. This reminded me of how important spiritual disciplines are in helping me to remain faithful.

Prayer: *O Holy One, help us remain connected to you so we might bear much fruit. We want to be your disciples and show our Father's glory. Amen*

Thought for the day: What practices keep me connected to Christ?

Betty L. Wigal (West Virginia, US)

A Dangerous Habit

Read 1 John 1:5–9

If we confess our sins, he who is faithful and just will forgive us our sins and cleanse us from all unrighteousness.
1 John 1:9 (NRSV)

I spent a week in a village by the sea. The air was fresh and pleasant, the sun and the sea were warm, and the surroundings were peaceful. When I returned home to Moscow, I wanted to cover my nose at the railway station. The smell of car exhaust fumes and drunken people attacked my nostrils. The air in Moscow was terrible. I longed for the fresh air by the sea. However, a week later, I no longer noticed the difference. I got used to the city air, which seemed completely normal, though it was actually harmful.

When we first encounter a sin in our lives, our reaction may be like mine at the railway station. The danger is that as we ignore our own sin, we no longer sense the stench of sin in our life. It seems normal. Failing to see the sin, however, does not remove its harmful consequences. But God promises that if we confess our sins we will be forgiven and made whole.

Prayer: *Dear Lord, thank you for your mercy in forgiving our sins. Holy Spirit, bring us the fresh breeze of grace that cleanses us from all unrighteousness. Amen*

Thought for the day: Confession can renew our souls.

Pavel Serdukov (Moscow, Russia)

Third Time Around

Read Psalm 31:1–5

God is faithful; by him you were called into the fellowship of his Son, Jesus Christ our Lord.
1 Corinthians 1:9 (NRSV)

Eleven years ago when my mother-in-law had breast cancer surgery, radiotherapy and chemotherapy, she declared after all the treatments were complete, 'Now I know that God is able.' She turned each fear and worry over to God and discovered his strength to be sufficient for her.

When her cancer returned, she told us, 'Yes, I know God is faithful.' Our family marvelled at how God's Spirit moved within her to bring her healing again. She has lived a long life of faith, but her witness to God's faithfulness intensified as she shared it with doctors, nurses and families of other oncology patients. Now my mother-in-law is undergoing treatments for her third round of breast cancer. Her serious situation breaks my heart.

Yet, in spite of the suffering and pain—and all the emotions that go with these difficulties—our family has witnessed first-hand God's power and faithfulness. With renewed hope I find myself asking, 'What will we discover about God this third time around?' Simply asking that question brings comfort. Indeed God is with us.

Prayer: *We thank you, dear God, because you make yourself known to us in joy and sorrow. Give us courage to trust in your presence with us during all circumstances. Amen*

Thought for the day: God is present in surprising ways.

Michelle Knight (Indiana, US)

Small Group Questions

Wednesday 7 May

1. Who taught you to pray? When do you first remember praying? What form did your prayers take?

2. Have you met a 'Harold'? A person who taught you a new and different way to pray? What did you like about this new way of praying? What was challenging about it?

3. Have you ever been a member of a prayer group? How did you find this group? What made you want to join? What is special to you about praying with a group? What is difficult?

4. When you hear others pray, what do you notice about their prayers? What do you want to do differently when you pray?

5. If you were asked to teach someone to pray, how would you do it? What would you tell them about prayer? What prayers would you teach them?

Wednesday 14 May

1. What experience do you have with autism? Has someone you love been diagnosed with autism or Asperger's Syndrome? How did you feel when you heard the news? How did you try to support that person and his or her family?

2. How does living with a chronic or incurable condition change your life? How does it affect the people around you?

3. How does your church or community support and include people who have special needs? How could your church or community be better at supporting and including these people?

4. Recall a time when you faced great adversity. What obstacles did you face? What helped you to persevere? What did you learn from that experience?

5. When have you been blessed by God in a surprising way? Why was it surprising to you? How did you recognise this blessing? How did this experience affect your faith?

6. Do you think Anthony's prayers were answered in the way he originally hoped? What is it like when your prayers are answered differently from what you had hoped or expected?

Wednesday 21 May

1. Recall a time in your childhood when you were afraid. What were you afraid of? How did you deal with this fear? If you confided in someone, who was it and how did they comfort you?

2. How have your fears changed throughout your life? What do you fear now? How do you deal with fears now? Whom do you confide in, and how do they help you?

3. If a frightened child came to you, how would you comfort them? What would you say or do?

4. How does your faith give you strength or courage when you are fearful? What spiritual practices or prayers help you to face your fears?

5. How does your church deal with fear? When times are uncertain financially or otherwise, what does your church do? What message does your pastor or minister preach? How does your church encourage you to face your fears or find strength in your faith during fearful times?

Wednesday 28 May

1. Have you had an experience like this one, where watching a video or looking at photos brought back important memories? What details had you forgotten? Looking back, why was this event or moment significant and worth remembering?

2. In addition to the examples from scripture that Mark lists, what other rituals or commands has God established to help us remember the meaning and history of our faith?

3. What rituals have been most meaningful to you and your spiritual journey? Is there one particular worship service, celebration of Communion, baptism or other ritual that stands out to you as being personally moving and powerful? Describe this experience.

4. How do you help your family or members of your community remember significant events? Do you have rituals or practices that help you pass these memories on to younger generations?

5. Read Deuteronomy 11:18–20. How does your church or community encourage children in their faith? How do you include children and young people in worship and the leadership of the church? What more could you do to include them and encourage them in their spiritual journeys?

Wednesday 4 June

1. When have you struggled financially? What was hardest about not having enough money? What changes did you have to make to your lifestyle or habits to make ends meet?

2. Who did you tell about your financial struggles? Was it difficult or easy to tell others about your need or ask for help? How did they respond?

3. When someone tells you they are struggling financially, how do you respond? What kinds of help do you offer?

4. Recall a time when you offered someone (or someone offered you) a piece of advice or scripture verse that was intended to be comforting but was not actually helpful. What did you learn from this experience? How will you offer advice or comfort to others in the future?

5. Sue writes that 'God works through us to do his will on earth.' What does this look like? How does your church or community strive to live out this vision?

Wednesday 11 June

1. Peter described looking forward to retirement and having a vision for what that new phase of his life would look like. Recall a time when you looked forward to a new life stage. What were you most excited about? What were you dreading? How did the reality match your vision for that life stage?

2. Do you know someone who has recently retired? If so, have you talked with them about the changes in their life? How might you encourage them to explore new activities and use their gifts?

3. What activities and responsibilities are most fulfilling for you? Which ones help you feel closer to God? Which ones are most draining? Why do you commit to these activities? What new activities would you like to try?

4. When you are facing a major change in your life, what makes you anxious? What makes you excited? How do you deal with big changes? What resources or practices help you to deal with major life changes?

5. When has your church or community undergone significant change? Were those changes painful, exciting, difficult or refreshing? How did your community handle these changes and feelings? What was helpful about this process? What could be done differently in the future to make the transition easier?

Wednesday 18 June

1. Do you know someone like Ruby who has a gift for being a carer? Describe this person's gifts and what you most admire about them.

2. When have you cared for someone and expected nothing in return? How did this experience affect you? What made it difficult? What encouraged you to continue?

3. In 1 Corinthians 11:1, Paul writes, 'Be imitators of me, as I am of Christ.' What does it mean to imitate Christ? How do you try to imitate Christ in your life?

4. How does your church support carers? What support does your church offer to care for those who are housebound? What other people or groups of people might need extra support from the community?

5. When you are busy caring for others or with work and family responsibilities, how do you care for yourself? What activities or practices help you to remain spiritually nourished? How will you take time to care for yourself this week?

6. Have you experienced having a 'love of your life' like Ruby? Who are the people in your life for whom you could be a servant in such a faithful way? Does love make such situations any easier?

Wednesday 25 June

1. When you are discouraged, where do you turn for encouragement? Who has provided encouragement to you in your spiritual journey?

2. Romans 15:4 tells us, 'For whatever was written in former days was written for our instruction, so that by steadfastness and by the encouragement of the scriptures we might have hope.' What scripture passages are the most encouraging for you? Why?

3. What has Christian community meant to you over the years? How has spending time with other Christians challenged your faith? How has it encouraged and supported your faith?

4. When you are discouraged, do you seek out others for prayer? Do you spend time alone in prayer? How has prayer been a source of support or encouragement for you or for someone you know?

5. Veronica writes that as fellow Christians we comfort one another, rejoice together, and hold each other accountable. What does it mean to hold another Christian accountable? Recall a time someone held you accountable in your spiritual life. What was helpful or challenging about that experience?

Wednesday 2 July

1. Is Sandra's experience familiar to you? When have you made assumptions about someone and later learned your assumptions were wrong? How did you feel? What did you do?

2. Recall a time when someone made hasty assumptions about you. What were those assumptions? Were they accurate? How did those assumptions make you feel? What did you do? How did the other person respond?

3. Read Mark 14:3–9. What assumptions do the onlookers make about the woman who anoints Jesus? How does Jesus respond? What lesson do you take from this story?

4. Sandra reminds us that everyone has a story. In your experience, what encourages you to share your story with others? How can you give others space and support to share their stories with you?

5. Does your church or faith community encourage people to share their stories with one another? Does your community reach out to strangers to learn their stories? If not, why? If so, how could you expand this practice?

Wednesday 9 July

1. When have you felt called to 'go over to the other side'? What were you called to do? Did you do it? Did you pray about your decision?

2. What types of ministries or outreach programmes have you experienced or heard about that stretch you beyond your comfort zone? Why do these ministries make you uncomfortable? What encouragement would you need to participate?

3. What risk has your church taken recently? How did those involved feel about taking the risk? How was God involved in the decision to take these risks? What was the outcome?

4. The disciples demonstrate courage when they leave their homes to follow Jesus. What new experience, adventure, or leap of faith would you like to have the courage to try? How are you seeking God's guidance as you long for this courage?

Wednesday 16 July

1. Recall a time when you read a Bible story and felt inspired to do something different because of it. What was the reading? Why was it inspiring to you in that moment? How did you act on your inspiration?

2. What does 'putting the word of God into practice' mean to you? What actions or spiritual practices help you to practise God's word?

3. Think of someone who you think practises God's word. What does this person do, think or say that demonstrates their faith? What one practice or example could you adopt to make your own life a demonstration of your faith?

4. When you have an important decision to make, how do you discern the right way forward? How does your faith inform your decision-making? Does the Bible guide you as you make decisions? How?

Wednesday 23 July

1. What experience do you have with cancer? Have you or a loved one been diagnosed with cancer? What was your initial reaction?

2. How has your relationship with God changed or been affected by traumatic experiences? What role has your faith played in bringing you through these experiences? What do you pray when you feel your world has been turned upside down?

3. Read Philippians 2:6–8. What does it mean to you that God became human in the person of Jesus Christ? How does this knowledge help you or change your perspective when you experience hardships?

4. Do you know someone who is struggling with cancer or another life-threatening illness? How can you support or encourage him/her during this time?

5. Deborah reached out to others with new understanding after her cancer diagnosis. What wounds or experiences have prepared you to reach out to others with compassion?

Wednesday 30 July

1. Xavia's childhood experience on the farm prepared her for the event she writes about in today's meditation. What childhood experiences have uniquely prepared you for particular events or parts of your adult life? Describe one of these experiences.

2. What messages or voices compete with God's voice in your life? Where do you hear these messages? How do you reconcile your faith with these competing messages?

3. How do you focus on God's voice in your life? What spiritual practices help you to feel connected to him?

4. Who in your life has helped you to recognise and follow God's leading? Describe this person and the ways they helped you live your faith.

5. How does your faith community help you to remain focused on God's guidance? What ministries, activities or traditions encourage you when you struggle to feel connected to God?

Wednesday 6 August

1. What was your reaction to reading Avon's story? What experiences have you had that allow you to relate to his experience?

2. Bullying happens in many settings. Have you or a loved one experienced bullying? How has your faith informed your perspective on the experience of bullying? How did you deal with the situation? Who did you call on for help?

3. Read Matthew 7:12. How easy or difficult do you find it to practise the principle in this verse? When is it easiest? When is it hardest? In what situations do you think living this verse is most important?

4. Recall a time when you felt that God transformed your heart. Describe that transformation. What did you feel inspired to do or do differently after that experience? Has that transformation been a lasting one?

5. Have you or your church participated in a ministry to prisoners? If so, what was that experience like? How did it change or inspire you? How did the ministry make a difference for the prisoners?

Wednesday 13 August

1. What do you do when you are discouraged? Do you seek solutions to your problems or distractions? To whom do you turn for encouragement and perspective?

2. When you feel discouraged, what scripture readings, hymns or prayers do you turn to? Do you remember when or how you discovered these? Describe why these readings, hymns or prayers give you comfort and encourage you.

3. Mary describes how burdens can be lightened when we talk about them with others. When have you experienced your own burdens being lightened in this way? When have you lightened someone else's burdens by listening?

4. Read Galatians 6:2. What does this verse mean to you? What does it look like to fulfil the law of Christ by bearing one another's burdens?

Wednesday 20 August

1. Cynthia describes the frustration of seeing mistakes flow from one generation to the next. What mistakes, poor choices or regrets have affected your family? How does your family acknowledge or talk about them? How has your family sought healing?

2. What traditions or religious practices has your family passed down through the generations? How do these traditions unify your family? How have they affected your personal faith and spiritual formation?

3. Read Isaiah 43:18–21. Describe a time when you experienced God doing a new thing in your life, in your family or in your community. How did this experience deepen or change your relationship with the people around you and with God?

4. How is your church passing down faith and wisdom to the next generations? How do you include children and young people in worship, in church activities and in outreach?

Wednesday 27 August

1. What do you think of Denise's response to her friend's troubles? How do you respond when people describe their problems to you? How do you feel?

2. When you feel overwhelmed by circumstances in your life, how do you want people to respond to you? What kinds of responses are most helpful and encouraging? Which responses are most unhelpful or discouraging?

3. When you pray, do you use scripture as a model or a starting point? If so, what are your favourite passages, prayers or examples? If not, why?

4. How does your church community listen to the needs of others? How does your community pray for those who are hurting? What do you like or dislike about the way your church listens and prays? How would you like to see these practices expanded or changed?

5. Describe an experience where someone's prayers made a difference in your life. How did this affect your understanding of prayer? How did it affect your personal prayer practice?

Hilda of Whitby

A spirituality for now

Ray Simpson

In the dark and turbulent centuries after the Roman occupation of Britain and during the Anglo-Saxon colonisation, the light of heaven still shone through the work and witness of the monastic communities, 'villages of God', which dotted the land. One of the most remarkable figures of those times was Hilda of Whitby. Born and reared among warring pagan tribes, through the influence of Celtic saints and scholars she became a dominant figure in the development of the British Church, above all at the famous Synod where Celtic and Roman Churches came together. Until recently, though, the story of this extraordinary woman has not received much attention.

Published to coincide with the 1400th anniversary of her birth, this book not only explores the drama of Hilda's life and ministry but shows what spiritual lessons we can draw for Christian life and leadership today.

ISBN 978 1 84101 728 0   £7.99
To order a copy of this book, please turn to the order form on page 159.

Also available for Kindle.

52 Reflections on Faith for Busy Preachers and Teachers

Stephen W. Need

These 52 reflections—one for each week of the year—provide short, sharp and profound insights into Christian faith and life. The aim is to stimulate thinking rather than provide all the answers, and show how faith can connect up with daily life, Bible teaching and also wider culture.

While the first half is based on themes of special relevance to Sundays throughout the Christian year, from Advent to the feast of Christ the King, the second half of the book considers core aspects of Christian belief, starting with God and ending with the risen Jesus on the Emmaus road. Offering a wealth of personal inspiration for preachers as well as stimulating material for group or individual study, the book makes an excellent ordination, commissioning or licensing gift.

ISBN 978 1 84101 743 3   £12.99

To order a copy of this book, please turn to the order form on page 159.

Also available for Kindle.

Creating a Life with God

The call of ancient prayer practices

Daniel Wolpert

Are you longing to take your relationship with God to a new level? This book introduces you to twelve prayer practices that:

- invite you to solitude and silence
- invite you to use your mind and imagination
- invite you to use your body and your creativity
- invite you to connect with nature and community

You'll meet 'travelling companions' from history, such as Ignatius Loyola and Julian of Norwich—individuals and groups whose lives were illuminated by these ways of praying. An appendix offers step-by-step instructions for practising the Jesus Prayer and the prayer of examen, for walking a labyrinth, praying with your body, and more—whether individually or as a group.

ISBN 978 0 85746 244 2   £7.99
To order a copy of this book, please turn to the order form on page 159.

Creative Prayer Ideas

A resource for church and group use

Claire Daniel

Prayer is a vital part of the Christian life but people often struggle with actually getting on and doing it. This book offers 80 imaginative and creative ideas for setting up 'prayer stations', practical ways of praying that involve the senses— touching, tasting, smelling, seeing, and hearing, rather than simply reflecting—as we bring our hopes, fears, dreams and doubts to God.

Developed from material tried and tested with small groups, the ideas provide activities ranging from bubble prayers to clay pot prayers (via just about everything else in between), and have been designed to be used with grown-ups of all ages.

ISBN 978 1 84101 688 7   £8.99

To order a copy of this book, please turn to the order form on page 159.

Also available for Kindle.

Bible Reading Resources Pack

Thank you for reading BRF Bible reading notes. BRF has been producing a variety of Bible reading notes for over 90 years, helping people all over the UK and the world connect with the Bible on a personal level every day.

Could you help us find other people who would enjoy our notes?

We produce a Bible Reading Resource Pack for church groups to use to encourage regular Bible reading.

This FREE pack contains:

- Samples of all BRF Bible reading notes.
- Our Resources for Personal Bible Reading catalogue, providing all you need to know about our Bible reading notes.
- A ready-to-use church magazine feature about BRF notes.
- Ready-made sermon and all-age service ideas to help your church into the Bible (ideal for Bible Sunday events).
- And much more!

How to order your FREE pack:

- Visit: www.biblereadingnotes.org.uk/request-a-bible-reading-resources-pack/
- Telephone: 01865 319700
- Post: Complete the form below and post to: Bible Reading Resource Pack, BRF, 15 The Chambers, Vineyard, Abingdon, OX14 3FE

Name...

Address ....

....Postcode..

Telephone ....

Email...

Please send me................................Bible Reading Resources Pack(s).

This pack is produced free of charge for all UK addresses but, if you wish to offer a donation towards our costs, this would be appreciated. If you require a pack to be sent outside of the UK, please contact us for details of postage and packing charges. Tel: +44 1865 319700. Thank you.

BRF is a Registered Charity

Subscriptions

The Upper Room is published in January, May and September.

Individual subscriptions

The subscription rate for orders for 4 or fewer copies includes postage and packing: THE UPPER ROOM annual individual subscription   £15.00

Church subscriptions

Orders for 5 copies or more, sent to ONE address, are post free:
THE UPPER ROOM annual church subscription   £11.85

Please do not send payment with order for a church subscription. We will send an invoice with your first order.

Please note that the annual billing period for church subscriptions runs from 1 May to 30 April.

Copies of the notes may also be obtained from Christian bookshops.

Single copies of *The Upper Room* will cost £3.95. Prices valid until 30 April 2015.

Giant print version

The Upper Room is available in giant print for the visually impaired, from:

Torch Trust for the Blind
Torch House
Torch Way,
Northampton Road
Market Harborough
LE16 9HL

Tel: 01858 438260
www.torchtrust.org

Individual Subscriptions

☐ I would like to take out a subscription myself (complete your name and address details only once)

☐ I would like to give a gift subscription (please complete both name and address sections below)

Your name...

Your address...

....Postcode.....................................

Your telephone number...

Gift subscription name..

Gift subscription address...

....Postcode.....................................

Gift message (20 words max)...

....

Please send *The Upper Room* beginning with the September 2014 / January 2015 / May 2015 issue: (delete as applicable)

THE UPPER ROOM ☐ £15.00

Please complete the payment details below and send, with appropriate payment, to: BRF, 15 The Chambers, Vineyard, Abingdon OX14 3FE

Total enclosed £.......... (cheques should be made payable to 'BRF')

Payment by ☐ cheque ☐ postal order ☐ Visa ☐ Mastercard ☐ Switch

Card no: ☐☐☐☐☐☐☐☐☐☐☐☐☐☐☐☐☐☐☐☐

Expires: ☐☐☐☐ Security code: ☐☐☐

Issue no (Switch): ☐☐☐☐

Signature (essential if paying by credit/Switch card) ....

☐ Please do not send me further information about BRF publications

☐ Please send me a Bible reading resources pack to encourage Bible reading in my church

BRF is a Registered Charity

Church Subscriptions

☐ Please send me ... copies of *The Upper Room* September 2014 / January 2015 / May 2015 issue (delete as applicable)

Name...

Address ....

....Postcode...

Telephone ....

Email..

Please send this completed form to:
BRF, 15 The Chambers, Vineyard, Abingdon OX14 3FE

Please do not send payment with this order. We will send an invoice with your first order.

Christian bookshops: All good Christian bookshops stock BRF publications. For your nearest stockist, please contact BRF.

Telephone: The BRF office is open between 09.15 and 17.30. To place your order, telephone 01865 319700; fax 01865 319701.

Web: Visit www.brf.org.uk

☐ Please send me a Bible reading resources pack to encourage Bible reading in my church

BRF is a Registered Charity

ORDERFORM

REF	TITLE	PRICE	QTY	TOTAL
728 0	Hilda of Whitby	£7.99		
743 3	52 Reflections on Faith…	£12.99		
244 2	Creating a Life with God	£7.99		
688 7	Creative Prayer Ideas	£8.99		

POSTAGE AND PACKING CHARGES				
Order value	UK	Europe	Surface	Air Mail
Under £7.00	£1.25	£3.00	£3.50	£5.50
£7.01–£29.99	£2.25	£5.50	£6.50	£10.00
Over £30.00	FREE	prices on request		

Postage and packing	
Donation	
TOTAL	

Name _____ Account Number _____

Address _____

_____ Postcode _____

Telephone Number_____

Email _____

Payment by: ❑ Cheque ❑ Mastercard ❑ Visa ❑ Postal Order ❑ Maestro

Card no ❑❑❑❑ ❑❑❑❑ ❑❑❑❑ ❑❑❑❑ ❑❑❑

Valid from ❑❑❑❑ Expires ❑❑❑❑ Issue no. ❑❑❑

Security code* ❑❑❑ *Last 3 digits on the reverse of the card.
ESSENTIAL IN ORDER TO PROCESS YOUR ORDER

Shaded boxes for Maestro use only

Signature _____ Date _____

All orders must be accompanied by the appropriate payment.

Please send your completed order form to:
BRF, 15 The Chambers, Vineyard, Abingdon OX14 3FE
Tel. 01865 319700 / Fax. 01865 319701 Email: enquiries@brf.org.uk

❑ Please send me further information about BRF publications.

Available from your local Christian bookshop.   BRF is a Registered Charity

About
brf:

BRF is a registered charity and also a limited company, and has been in existence since 1922. Through all that we do—producing resources, providing training, working face-to-face with adults and children, and via the web—we work to resource individuals and church communities in their Christian discipleship through the Bible, prayer and worship.

Our Barnabas children's team works with primary schools and churches to help children under 11, and the adults who work with them, to explore Christianity creatively and to bring the Bible alive.

To find out more about BRF and its core activities and ministries, visit:

www.brf.org.uk
www.brfonline.org.uk
www.biblereadingnotes.org.uk
www.barnabasinschools.org.uk
www.barnabasinchurches.org.uk
www.faithinhomes.org.uk
www.messychurch.org.uk
www.foundations21.net

If you have any questions about BRF and our work, please email us at

enquiries@brf.org.uk